WORLD ENGLISH 1

SECOND EDITION

Real People • Real Places • Real Language

Martin Milner, Author

Rob Jenkins, Series Editor

NATIONAL GEOGRAPHIC LEARNING | **CENGAGE Learning**

Australia • Brazil • Japan • Korea • Mexico • Singapore • Spain • United Kingdom • United States

World English Level 1
Real People, Real Places, Real Language
Martin Milner, Author
Rob Jenkins, Series Editor

Publisher: Sherrise Roehr

Executive Editor: Sarah Kenney

Senior Development Editor: Margarita Matte

Development Editor: Brenden Layte

Assistant Editor: Alison Bruno

Editorial Assistant: Patricia Giunta

Media Researcher: Leila Hishmeh

Senior Technology Product Manager: Scott Rule

Director of Global Marketing: Ian Martin

Senior Product Marketing Manager:
  Caitlin Thomas

Sr. Director, ELT & World Languages:
  Michael Burggren

Production Manager: Daisy Sosa

Content Project Manager: Andrea Bobotas

Senior Print Buyer: Mary Beth Hennebury

Cover Designer: Aaron Opie

Art Director: Scott Baker

Creative Director: Chris Roy

Cover Image: Slow Images/Getty Images

Compositor: MPS Limited

Cover image

Church Nossa Senhora do Rosário dos Pretos, Salvador, Brazil

For product information and technology assistance, contact us at
Cengage Learning Customer & Sales Support, 1-800-354-9706

For permission to use material from this text or product,
submit all requests online at **cengage.com/permissions**
Further permissions questions can be emailed to
permissionrequest@cengage.com

World English Level 1 ISBN: 978-1-285-84869-3
World English Level 1 + CD-ROM ISBN: 978-1-285-84835-8
World English Level 1 + Online Workbook ISBN: 978-1-305-08954-9

National Geographic Learning
20 Channel Center Street
Boston, MA 02210
USA

Cengage Learning is a leading provider of customized learning solutions with office locations around the globe, including Singapore, the United Kingdom, Australia, Mexico, Brazil, and Japan.

Cengage Learning products are represented in Canada by Nelson Education, Ltd.

Visit National Geographic Learning online at ngl.cengage.com

Visit our corporate website at www.cengage.com

Printed in the United States of America
6 7 8 9 10   19 18 17 16

Thank you to the educators who provided invaluable feedback during the development of the second edition of the *World English* series:

AMERICAS

Brazil

Renata Cardoso, Universidade de Brasília, Brasília
Gladys De Sousa, Universidade Federal de Minas Gerais, Belo Horizonte
Marilena Fernandes, Associação Alumni, São Paulo
Mary Ruth Popov, Ingles Express, Ltda., Belo Horizonte
Ana Rosa, Speed, Vila Velha
Danny Sheps, English4u2, Natal
Renata Zainotte, Go Up Idiomas, Rio de Janeiro

Colombia

Eida Caicedo, Universidad de San Buenaventura Cali, Cali
Andres Felipe Echeverri Patiño, Corporación Universitaria Lasallista, Envigado
Luz Libia Rey, Centro Colombo Americano, Bogota

Dominican Republic

Aida Rosales, Instituto Cultural Dominico-Americano, Santo Domingo

Ecuador

Elizabeth Ortiz, COPFI-Copol English Institute, Guayaquil

Mexico

Ramon Aguilar, LEC Languages and Education Consulting, Hermosillo
Claudia García-Moreno Ávila, Universidad Autónoma del Estado de México, Toluca
Ana María Benton, Universidad Anahuac Mexico Norte, Huixquilucan
Martha Del Angel, Tecnológico de Monterrey, Monterrey
Sachenka García B., Universidad Kino, Hermosillo
Cinthia I. Navarrete García, Universidad Autónoma del Estado de México, Toluca
Alonso Gaxiola, Universidad Autonoma de Sinaloa, Guasave
Raquel Hernandez, Tecnológico de Monterrey, Monterrey
Beatriz Cuenca Hernández, Universidad Autónoma del Estado de México, Toluca
Luz María Lara Hernández, Universidad Autónoma del Estado de México, Toluca
Esthela Ramírez Hernández, Universidad Autónoma del Estado de México, Toluca
Ma Guadalupe Peña Huerta, Universidad Autónoma del Estado de México, Toluca
Elsa Iruegas, Prepa Tec Campus Cumbres, Monterrey
María del Carmen Turral Maya, Universidad Autónoma del Estado de México, Toluca
Lima Melani Ayala Olvera, Universidad Autónoma del Estado de México, Toluca
Suraya Ordorica Reyes, Universidad Autónoma del Estado de México, Toluca
Leonor Rosales, Tecnológico de Monterrey, Monterrey
Leticia Adelina Ruiz Guerrero, ITESO, Jesuit University, Tlaquepaque

United States

Nancy Alaks, College of DuPage, Glen Ellyn, IL
Annette Barker, College of DuPage, Aurora, IL
Joyce Gatto, College of Lake County, Grayslake, IL
Donna Glade-Tau, Harper College, Palatine, IL
Mary "Katie" Hu, Lone Star College – North Harris, Houston, TX
Christy Naghitorabi, University of South Florida, St. Petersburg, FL

ASIA

Beri Ali, Cleverlearn (American Academy), Ho Chi Minh City
Ronald Anderson, Chonnam National University, Yeosu Campus, Jeollanam
Michael Brown, Canadian Secondary Wenzhou No. 22 School, Wenzhou
Leyi Cao, Macau University of Science and Technology, Macau
Maneerat Chuaychoowong, Mae Fah Luang University, Chiang Rai
Sooah Chung, Hwarang Elementary School, Seoul
Edgar Du, Vanung University, Taoyuan County
David Fairweather, Asahikawa Daigaku, Asahikawa
Andrew Garth, Chonnam National University, Yeosu Campus, Jeollanam
Brian Gaynor, Muroran Institute of Technology, Muroran-shi
Emma Gould, Chonnam National University, Yeosu Campus, Jeollanam
David Grant, Kochi National College of Technology, Nankoku
Michael Halloran, Chonnam National University, Yeosu Campus, Jeollanam
Nina Ainun Hamdan, University Malaysia, Kuala Lumpur
Richard Hatcher, Chonnam National University, Yeosu Campus, Jeollanam
Edward Tze-Lu Ho, Chihlee Institute of Technology, New Taipei City
Soontae Hong, Yonsei University, Seoul
Chaiyathip Katsura, Mae Fah Luang University, Chiang Rai
Byoug-Kyo Lee, Yonsei University, Seoul
Han Li, Aceleader International Language Center, Beijing
Michael McGuire, Kansai Gaidai University, Osaka
Yu Jin Ng, Universiti Tenaga Nasional, Kajang, Selangor
Somaly Pan, Royal University of Phnom Penh, Phnom Penh
HyunSuk Park, Halla University, Wonju
Bunroeun Pich, Build Bright University, Phnom Penh
Renee Sawazaki, Surugadai University, Annaka-shi
Adam Schofield, Cleverlearn (American Academy), Ho Chi Minh City
Pawadee Srisang, Burapha University, Chanthaburi Campus, Ta-Mai District
Douglas Sweetlove, Kinjo Gakuin University, Nagoya
Tari Lee Sykes, National Taiwan University of Science and Technology, Taipei
Monika Szirmai, Hiroshima International University, Hiroshima
Sherry Wen, Yan Ping High School, Taipei
Chris Wilson, Okinawa University, Naha City, Okinawa
Christopher Wood, Meijo University, Nagoya
Evelyn Wu, Minghsin University of Science and Technology, Xinfeng, Hsinchu County
Aroma Xiang, Macau University of Science and Technology, Macau
Zoe Xie, Macau University of Science and Technology, Macau
Juan Xu, Macau University of Science and Technology, Macau
Florence Yap, Chang Gung University, Taoyuan
Sukanda Yatprom, Mae Fah Luang University, Chiang Rai
Echo Yu, Macau University of Science and Technology, Macau

The publisher would like to extend a special thank you to Raúl Billini, English Coordinator, Mi Colegio, Dominican Republic, for his contributions to the series.

BACKGROUND – LEARNING AND INSTRUCTION

Learning has been described as acquiring knowledge. Obtaining knowledge does not guarantee understanding, however. A math student, for example, could replicate any number of algebraic formulas, but never come to an *understanding* of how they could be used or for what purpose he or she has learned them. If understanding is defined as the ability to use knowledge, then learning could be defined differently and more accurately. The ability of the student to use knowledge instead of merely receiving information therefore becomes the goal and the standard by which learning is assessed.

This revelation has led to classrooms that are no longer teacher-centric or lecture driven. Instead, students are asked to think, ponder, and make decisions based on the information received or, even more productive, students are asked to construct learning or discover information in personal pursuits, or with help from an instructor, with partners, or in groups. The practice they get from such approaches stimulates learning with a purpose. The purpose becomes a tangible goal or objective that provides opportunities for students to transfer skills and experiences to future learning.

In the context of language development, this approach becomes essential to real learning and understanding. Learning a language is a skill that is developed only after significant practice. Students can learn the mechanics of a language but when confronted with real-world situations, they are not capable of communication. Therefore, it might be better to shift the discussion from "Language Learning" to "Communication Building." Communication should not be limited to only the productive skills. Reading and listening serve important avenues for communication as well.

FOUR PRINCIPLES TO DEVELOPING LEARNING ENVIRONMENTS

Mission: The goal or mission of a language course might adequately be stated as the pursuit of providing sufficient information and practice to allow students to communicate accurately and effectively to a reasonable extent given the level, student experiences, and time on task provided. This goal can be reflected in potential student learning outcomes identified by what students will be able to do through performance indicators.

World English provides a clear chart within the table of contents to show the expected outcomes of the course. The books are designed to capture student imagination and allow students ample opportunities to communicate. A study of the table of contents identifies the process of communication building that will go on during the course.

Context: It is important to identify what vehicle will be used to provide instruction. If students are to learn through practice, language cannot be introduced as isolated verb forms, nouns, and modifiers. It must have context. To reach the learners and to provide opportunities to communicate, the context must be interesting and relevant to learners' lives and expectations. In other words, there must be a purpose and students must have a clear understanding of what that purpose is.

World English provides a meaningful context that allows students to connect with the world. Research has demonstrated pictures and illustrations are best suited for creating interest and motivation within learners. National Geographic has a long history of providing magnificent learning environments through pictures, illustrations, true accounts, and video. The pictures, stories, and video capture the learners' imagination and "hook" them to learning in such a way that students have significant reasons to communicate promoting interaction and critical thinking. The context will also present students with a desire to know more, leading to life-long learning.

Objectives (Goals)

With the understanding that a purpose for communicating is essential, identifying precisely what the purpose is in each instance becomes crucial even before specifics of instruction have been defined. This is often called "backward design." Backward design means in the context of classroom lesson planning that first desired outcomes, goals, or objectives are defined and then lessons are mapped out with the end in mind, the end being what students will be able to do after sufficient instruction and practice. Having well-crafted objectives or goals provides the standard by which learners' performance can be assessed or self-assessed.

World English lessons are designed on two-page spreads so students can easily see what is expected and what the context is. The goal that directly relates to the final application activity is identified at the beginning. Students, as well as instructors, can easily evaluate their performance as they attempt the final activity. Students can also readily see what tools they will practice to prepare them for the application activity. The application activity is a task where students can demonstrate their ability to perform what the lesson goal requires. This information provides direction and purpose for the learner. Students, who know what is expected, where they are going, and how they will get there, are more apt to reach success. Each success builds confidence and additional communication skills.

Tools and Skills

Once the lesson objective has been identified and a context established, the lesson developer must choose the tools the learner will need to successfully perform the task or objective. The developer can choose among various areas in communication building including vocabulary, grammar and pronunciation. The developer must also choose skills and strategies including reading, writing, listening, and speaking. The receptive skills of reading and listening are essential components to communication. All of these tools and skills must be placed in a balanced way into a context providing practice that can be transferred to their final application or learner demonstration which ultimately becomes evidence of communication building.

World English units are divided into "lessons" that each consists of a two-page spread. Each spread focuses on different skills and strategies and is labeled by a letter (A-E). The units contain the following lesson sequence:

> A: Vocabulary
> B: Listening and Pronunciation
> C: Language Expansion
> D: Reading/Writing
> E: Video Journal

Additional grammar and vocabulary are introduced as tools throughout to provide practice for the final application activity. Each activity in a page spread has the purpose of developing adequate skills to perform the final application task.

LAST WORD

The philosophy of World English is to provide motivating context to connect students to the world through which they build communication skills. These skills are developed, practiced, and assessed from lesson to lesson through initially identifying the objective and giving learners the tools they need to complete a final application task. The concept of performance is highlighted over merely learning new information and performance comes from communicating about meaningful and useful context. An accumulation of small communication skills leads to true and effective communication outside of the classroom in real-world environments.

		Unit Goals	Grammar	Vocabulary
UNIT 1	**People** Page 2	• Meet people • Ask for and give personal information • Describe different occupations • Describe positive and negative parts of occupations	Review of Present tense: *Be* *Be* + adjective (+ noun) Possessive adjectives	Occupations Countries Nationalities Descriptive adjectives
UNIT 2	**Work, Rest, and Play** Page 14	• Talk about a typical day • Talk about free time • Describe a special celebration or festival • Describe daily life in different communities	Review: Simple present tense Prepositions of time Adverbs of frequency	Daily activities Party words Celebrations and festivals
UNIT 3	**Going Places** Page 26	• Identify possessions • Ask for and give personal travel information • Give travel advice • Share special travel tips with others	Possession Imperatives and *should* for advice	Travel preparations and stages Ordinal numbers Travel documents and money

TEDTALKS Video Page 38 **Eric Whitacre: A Virtual Choir 2,000 Voices Strong**

		Unit Goals	Grammar	Vocabulary
UNIT 4	**Food** Page 42	• Give a recipe • Order a meal • Talk about diets • Discuss unusual foods	Count and non-count nouns: *some* and *any* *How much* and *How many* with quantifiers: *lots of, a few, a little*	Food Food groups Diets
UNIT 5	**Sports** Page 54	• Describe activities happening now • Compare everyday and present-time activities • Talk about favorite sports • Discuss adventures	Present continuous tense Stative verbs	Doing sports Present-time activities Team sports and individual sports
UNIT 6	**Destinations** Page 66	• Discuss past vacations • Exchange information about vacations • Use *was/were* to describe a personal experience • Describe a discovery from the past	Simple past tense Simple past tense of *to be*	Travel activities Emphatic adjectives

TEDTALKS Video Page 78 **Lewis Pugh: My Mind-Shifting Everest Swim**

Listening	Speaking and Pronunciation	Reading	Writing	Video Journal
Focused listening: Personal introductions	Asking for and giving personal information Contractions of *be*: *–'m, –'re, –'s*	**National Geographic:** "People from Around the World"	Writing about people's occupations and nationalities	**National Geographic:** "The Last of The Woman Divers"
Focused listening: A radio celebrity interview	Talking about daily schedules and free time Verbs that end in *–s*	**TED**TALKS "Eric Whitacre: A Virtual Choir 2,000 Voices Strong"	Writing a descriptive paragraph about daily routines Writing Strategy: Word web	**National Geographic:** "Monkey Business"
General listening: Conversations at travel destinations	Giving personal information for travel forms Rising intonation on lists	**National Geographic:** "Smart Traveler"	Writing travel tips	**National Geographic:** "Beagle Patrol"
General and focused listening: Ordering a meal in a restaurant	Role-play: Purchasing food at a supermarket Reduced forms: *Do you have . . .* and *Would you like . . .*	**National Geographic:** "Bugs as Food"	Writing a recipe	**National Geographic:** "Dangerous Dinner"
General and focused listening: Everyday activities vs. today's activities	Talking about what people are doing now Discussing favorite sports Reduced form: *What are you . . .*	**TED**TALKS "Lewis Pugh: My Mind-Shifting Everest Swim"	Writing an e-mail	**National Geographic:** "Cheese-Rolling Races"
General listening: A vacation	Comparing vacations Describing personal experiences Sounds of *–ed* endings	**National Geographic:** "The Cradle of the Inca Empire"	Writing a travel blog	**National Geographic:** "Machu Picchu"

		Unit Goals	Grammar	Vocabulary
UNIT 7	**Communication** Page 82	• Talk about personal communication • Exchange contact information • Describe characteristics and qualities • Compare different types of communication	Verbs with direct and indirect objects Irregular past tense Sensory verbs	Communication Electronics The senses
UNIT 8	**Moving Forward** Page 94	• Talk about plans • Discuss long- and short-term plans • Make weather predictions • Discuss the future	Future tense: *be going to* *Will* for predictions and immediate decisions	Short- and long-term plans Weather conditions Weather-specific clothing
UNIT 9	**Types of Clothing** Page 106	• Make comparisons • Explain preferences • Talk about clothing materials • Evaluate quality and value	Comparatives Superlatives	Clothing Descriptive adjectives Clothing materials

TEDTALKS Video Page 118 **Diana Reiss: Peter Gabriel, Neil Gershenfeld, Vint Cerf: The Interspecies Internet? An Idea in Progress**

		Unit Goals	Grammar	Vocabulary
UNIT 10	**Lifestyles** Page 122	• Give advice on healthy habits • Compare lifestyles • Ask about lifestyles • Evaluate your lifestyle	Modals (*could, ought to, should, must*); *have to* Questions with *how*	Healthy and unhealthy habits Compound adjectives
UNIT 11	**Achievements** Page 134	• Talk about today's chores • Interview for a job • Talk about personal accomplishments • Discuss humanity's greatest achievements	Present perfect tense Present perfect tense vs. simple past tense	Chores Personal accomplishments
UNIT 12	**Consequences** Page 146	• Talk about managing your money • Make choices on how to spend your money • Talk about cause and effect • Evaluate money and happiness	Real conditionals (also called the first conditional)	Personal finance Animals Animal habitats

TEDTALKS Video Page 158 **Michael Norton: How to Buy Happiness**

Listening	Speaking and Pronunciation	Reading	Writing	Video Journal
Focused listening: A radio call-in program	Asking for contact information Describing sights, sounds and other sensations The /b/ and /v/, /l/ and /r/ sounds	**TED**TALKS "Diana Reiss, Peter Gabriel, Neil Gershenfeld, Vint Cerf: The Interspecies Internet? An Idea in Progress"	Writing a text message Make a list	**National Geographic:** "Wild Animal Trackers"
General listening: A talk show	Talking about weekend plans Discussing the weather Reduced form of *going to*	**National Geographic:** "Future Energy"	Writing statements about the future	**National Geographic:** "Solar Cooking"
Focused listening: Shoe shopping	Talking about clothes Shopping—at the store and online Rising and falling intonation	**National Geographic:** "Silk—the Queen of Textiles"	Writing about buying clothes	**National Geographic:** "How Your T-Shirt Can Make a Difference"
General listening: Personal lifestyles	Discussing healthy and unhealthy habits Asking and telling about lifestyles *Should, shouldn't*	**National Geographic:** "The Secrets of Long Life"	Writing a paragraph about personal lifestyle	**National Geographic:** "The Science of Stress"
Listening for general understanding and specific details: A job interview	Interviewing for a job Catching up with a friend Reduced form of *have*	**National Geographic:** "Humanity's Greatest Achievements"	Writing about achievements	**National Geographic:** "Spacewalk"
Listening for specific details: At a travel agency Listening for key information	Making decisions about spending money Talking about important environmental issues Intonation, sentence stress	**TED**TALKS "Michael Norton: How to Buy Happiness"	Write about cause and effect Writing Strategy: Make suggestions	**National Geographic:** "The Missing Snows of Kilimanjaro"

A girl in a red dress stands out among Muslim women praying on the eve of Ramadan in East Java, Indonesia.

Look at the photo, answer the questions:

1 Who are these people?
Share your ideas with a partner.

2 Are they like you?
Why or why not?

UNIT 1 GOALS

1. Meet people

2. Ask for and give personal information

3. Describe different occupations

4. Describe positive and negative parts of occupations

3

GOAL 1: Meet People

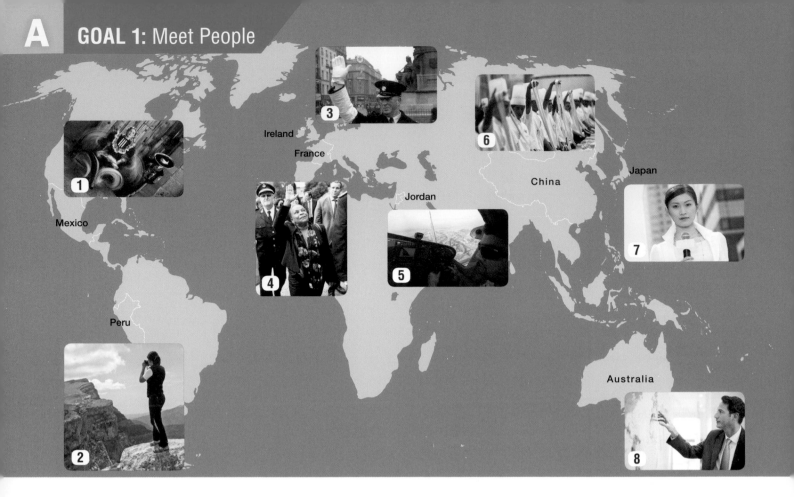

Countries and Nationalities

China — Chinese
Australia — Australian
Jordan — Jordanian
France — French
Mexico — Mexican
Peru — Peruvian
Ireland — Irish
Japan — Japanese

Engage!

Rank the occupations from most difficult (1) to least difficult (8).

Real Language

We say *What does she/he do* to ask about a person's occupation or job.

Occupations

~~dancer~~ pilot chef journalist politician
photographer police officer travel agent

Vocabulary

A Fill in the blanks. Use words from the boxes.

1. This is Norma. She's _____Mexican_____ and she's a _____dancer_____.
2. This is Gabriela. She's _____ and she's a _____.
3. This is Frank. He's _____ and he's a _____.
4. This is Marie. She's _____ and she's a _____.
5. This is Yaseen. He's _____ and he's a _____.
6. This is Chuan Li. He's _____ and he's a _____.
7. This is Nanako. She's _____ and she's a _____.
8. This is Nicolas. He's _____ and he's a _____.

B Work with a partner. Talk about the people in the pictures.

> Norma is from Mexico.

> Oh, she's Mexican. What does she do?

> She's a dancer.

Grammar: *Be*

Subject pronoun + *be*			*Be* contractions	
I **am**			**I'm**	
You/We/They **are**		Thai.	**You're** **We're** **They're**	Thai.
He/She/It **is**			**He's** **She's** **It's**	

Negative statements with *be*			
Subject pronoun	**Be**	**Negative**	
I	**am**		a dancer.
You/We/They	**are**	not	dancers.
He/She/It	**is**		a dancer.

Yes/No questions			
Be	**Pronoun**		**Short answers**
Are	you/they	Mexican?	Yes, I **am.** No, I**'m** not.
Is	he/she/it		Yes, they **are.** No, he **isn't.**

A Match the questions and the answers.

1. Are you a doctor? _____
2. Is she Chinese? _____
3. Is Ben Australian? _____
4. Are Mario and Teresa students? _____

a. Yes, he is.
b. No, she isn't. She's Japanese.
c. Yes, they are. They're from Argentina.
d. No, I'm not. I'm a nurse.

B Fill in the blanks with a pronoun and the correct form of the verb *be*.

1. _____ from Japan. I'm from Thailand.
2. _____ from Indonesia? Yes, I am.
3. Where _____ from? They're from China.
4. _____ an engineer. He's a doctor.

Conversation

A 🔊 **2** Listen to the conversation. Where is Sean from?

Sean: So, Claudia, where are you from?
Claudia: I'm from <u>Chile</u>.
Sean: So, you're <u>Chilean</u>, eh? Sounds cool. Are you from <u>Santiago</u>?
Claudia: Yes, I am. And you, Sean? Where are you from?
Sean: I'm <u>Canadian</u>.
Claudia: Wow! <u>Canada</u>. I'd love to go to <u>Canada</u>. Which city are you from?
Sean: I'm from <u>Toronto</u>.

B 🗣 Practice the conversation with a partner. Switch roles and practice it again.

C 🗣 Change the underlined words and make a new conversation.

D ♣ **GOAL CHECK** ✔ **Meet people**

Choose an occupation, a nationality, and a country for yourself. Walk around the class and introduce yourself to other classmates.

Real Language

To show surprise and interest we can say:

Formal ←——→ **Informal**
Really?   *Wow!*   *Cool!*

Listening

A 🗨 Look at the pictures. Talk to a partner. Guess the missing information.

B 🔊 3 Listen to the TV game show. Fill in the blanks with the correct information.

1. Name: Kyoko Hashimoro

Nationality: _____

City: Tokyo

Country: Japan

Occupation: _____

3. Name: Jim Waters

Nationality: _____

City: Coldstone

Country: _____

Occupation: Farmer

2. Name: Luis Gomez

Nationality: _____

City: Lima

Country: _____

Occupation: _____

4. Name: Bianca da Silva

Nationality: _____

City: Rio de Janeiro

Country: _____

Occupation: Musician

C 🔊 3 Listen to the questions in the game show. Write the nationality.

1. Country: Jordan   **Nationality:** _____

2. Country: Germany   **Nationality:** _____

3. Country: Switzerland   **Nationality:** _____

4. Country: Jamaica   **Nationality:** _____

Pronunciation: Contractions of *be*

A 🔊 4 Listen and repeat.

1. I am   I'm

2. you are   you're

3. he is   he's

4. she is   she's

5. it is   it's

B 🔊 5 Listen. Circle the verb or contraction you hear. Then listen again and repeat.

1. ((I am) | I'm) a teacher.
2. (He is | He's) an engineer.
3. (She is | She's) a nurse.
4. (They are | They're) interesting.
5. (You are | You're) welcome.

C 👥 Play round-robin.

Student 1: I'm a dentist.

Student 2: I'm a student, and he's a dentist.

Student 3: I'm a teacher, she's a student, and he's a dentist.

Continue the game for as many occupations as possible.

Communication

A 🔄 **Student A** chooses a card from the ones to the right. **Student B** guesses the card by asking *yes/no* questions.

B: Are you 28 years old?   **A:** No, I'm not.

B: Are you a doctor?   **A:** Yes, I am.

B: Are you Argentinian?   **A:** No, I'm not.

B: Is your name Helen?   **A:** Yes, it is!

B 👥 Choose a famous person. The others in the group ask *yes/no* questions to guess who you are. They can ask 20 questions.

> Are you American?

> Yes, I am.

> Are you a man?

> No, I'm not.

C 👥 **GOAL CHECK** ✔ **Ask for and give personal information**

Interview some of your classmates. Ask their name, their age, and the job they do or want to do.

> What job do you want to do?

> I want to be a pilot.

▲ Andrew is a pilot.

Name: Andrew
Nationality: American
Age: 28
Job: Pilot

Name: Pablo
Nationality: Argentinian
Age: 28
Job: Doctor

Name: Mi Hi
Nationality: Korean
Age: 23
Job: Architect

Name: Helen
Nationality: American
Age: 30
Job: Doctor

Name: Kwan
Nationality: Korean
Age: 30
Job: Architect

Name: Ana
Nationality: Argentinian
Age: 23
Job: Teacher

Language Expansion: Descriptive adjectives

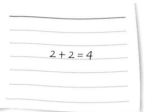

▲ easy

▲ happy

▲ unhappy

▲ interesting

▲ boring

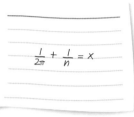

▲ difficult

▲ rich

▲ poor

▲ safe

▲ dangerous

A Write the words in the correct column.

Positive	Negative
happy	unhappy

Word Focus

salary = money earned through the work you do

Possessive Adjectives

This is **my** friend.

Is that **your** brother?

His/Her friend comes from Uruguay.

Their parents are nice people.

*Possessive nouns are formed with an apostrophe (') + -s. Laura's friend is from London.

B 🔁 Read the sentences. Circle an adjective. Compare your answer to your partner's. Discuss any differences.

1. Dan is a travel agent. His job is (interesting | boring).
2. Ana is a police officer. Her job is (safe | dangerous).
3. Mario's job does not have a good **salary.** He is (happy | unhappy).
4. Ismael is a doctor. He is (rich | poor).
5. Gabriela is a teacher. Her job is (easy | difficult).

Grammar: *Be* + adjective (+ noun)

Subject	*Be*	Adjective
My friend	**is**	rich.
His job	**is**	dangerous.
I	**am**	not happy.
My brother's job	**is**	interesting.

Subject	*Be*	Article	Adjective	Noun
It	**is**	an	easy	job.
Your friend	**is**	an	interesting	person.
It	**is**	a	difficult	life.

Victor is an environmentalist. His job is interesting and dangerous.

A Circle the correct word or phrase in parentheses.

1. My father's job is (interesting | an interesting). He is a newspaper photographer. It's not (easy | an easy) job, but he enjoys it.

2. I am a travel agent. The salary isn't very (good | an good). I'm not (rich | an rich).

3. John is an engineer. It's (difficult | a difficult) job, but it's (interesting | an interesting) job.

B Complete the sentences using a possessive adjective.

1. I am a farmer. _____ salary is not very good.

2. Michael is a musician. _____ job is interesting.

3. Susan and Jenny are from Ireland. _____ nationality is Irish.

4. You are a pilot. I think _____ job is dangerous.

5. Michelle is from Germany. _____ nationality is German.

C Unscramble the words to write sentences.

1. job   friend's   is   My   dangerous.   _____

2. is   person.   interesting   Kim's   friend   an   _____

3. your   happy?   brother   Is   _____

4. rich   is   not   a   My   father   man.   _____

Conversation

A 🔊 6 Listen to the conversation. What does Graham do?

Graham: What do you do, Elsa?
Elsa: I'm <u>an engineer</u>.
Graham: <u>An engineer</u>! That's interesting.
Elsa: Yes, but it's difficult work. And you, Graham? What do you do?

Graham: I'm <u>a policeman</u>.
Elsa: <u>A policeman</u>! Is it dangerous?
Graham: No. In fact, sometimes it's boring.

B 🔁 Practice the conversation with a partner. Switch roles and practice it again. Then change the underlined words and make a new conversation.

C 🔁 **GOAL CHECK** ✔ **Describe different occupations**
Choose an occupation and say two things to your partner about it. Take turns.

D GOAL 4: Describe Positive and Negative Parts of Occupations

Reading

A Look at the pictures. What do you think these people do?

B Read the article. Circle **T** for *true* and **F** for *false*.

1. Peter is a pilot. **T F**
2. Peter's salary is good. **T F**
3. Rimii is from India. **T F**
4. She says her work is sometimes interesting. **T F**
5. Tanya is an engineer. **T F**
6. She says school is difficult. **T F**

C Answer the questions.

1. What does Peter do?

   ____

2. Is Peter poor?

   ____

3. What does Rimii do?

   ____

4. Is her salary good?

   ____

5. Where is Tanya from?

   ____

6. Do you think Tanya is happy?

   ____

PEOPLE FROM AROUND THE WORLD

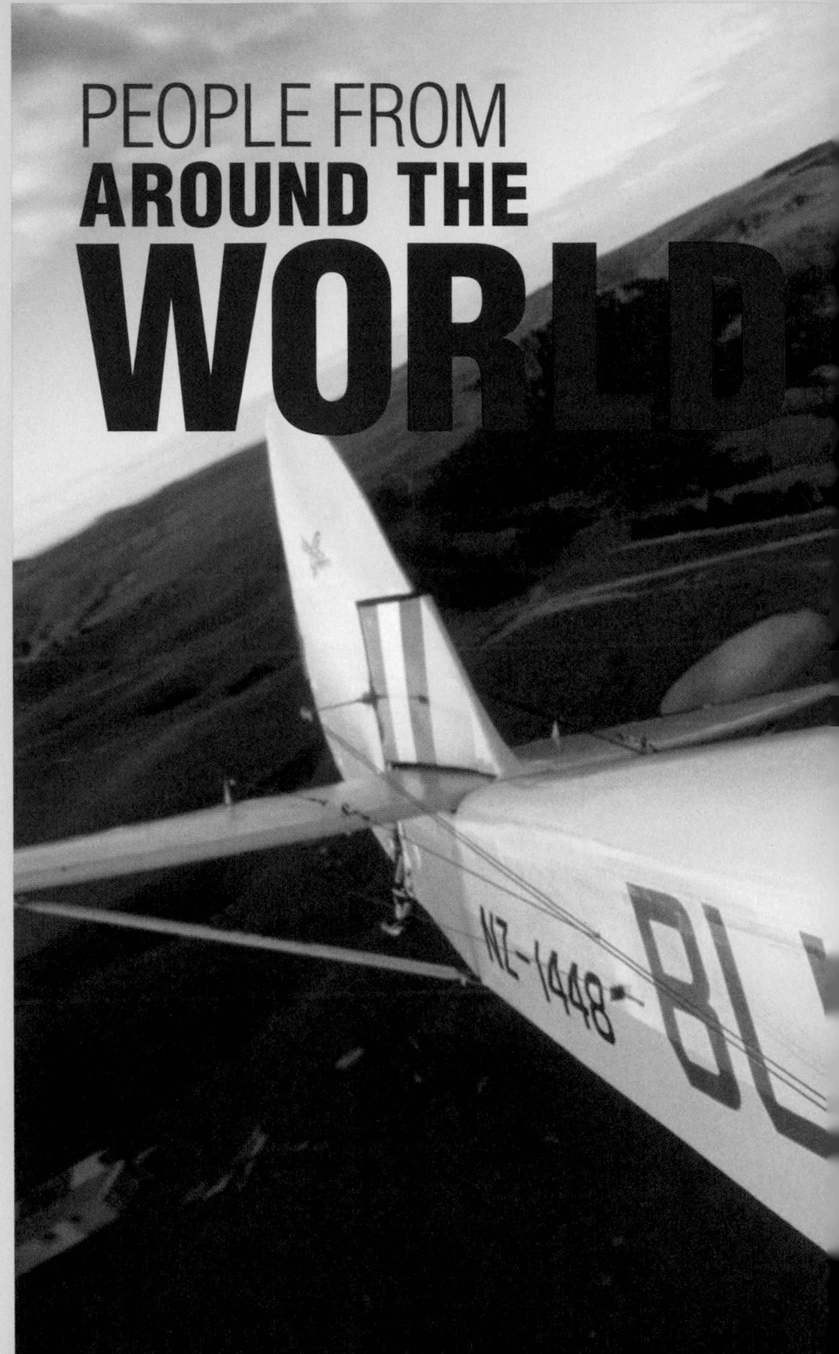

For some people, their job is interesting, but their salary is not good. For other people, their job is boring, but their salary is good. And then for some lucky people, their job is interesting, and their salary is good.

Let's look at some people and their jobs:

Peter Elworthy is from New Zealand. He is not a pilot; he's a farmer! His farm is very big,

FIRE
REAR C

so he uses an airplane. He says, "I'm happy. My job is interesting, and also the salary is good. And my dog, Shep, can come with me in the airplane."

Rimii Sen is an actress. She is Indian, and she is from Mumbai. "People think an actress's life is exciting, but it is difficult work, and sometimes it is boring. However, the salary is very good!"

Tanya Rogers is a student from Boulder, Colorado, in the United States. She is studying to be an engineer, but she really wants to be a musician. "School is boring, and I love my music. For some musicians, the salary is good, but for most musicians it is not good."

Engineer or musician? What a decision!

Safi

▲ Angeline

▲ Asef

Communication

A 🔄 With a partner, make a list of all the jobs you know. Individually, write them in the boxes in the chart below.

	Good salary	Poor salary
Interesting		*dancer*
Boring		

B 🔄 Compare your answers with your partner's.

Writing

A Look at the people. Write about each person's job and nationality.

Safi: Afghanistan

Safi is ___Afghani___ and _he is a farmer._____

Angeline: Brazil

Angeline is _____ and _____

Asef: Jordan

Asef is _____ and _____

B 🔄 **GOAL CHECK** ✓ **Describe positive and negative parts of occupations**

With a partner, talk about a friend or family member and his or her occupation. Describe good and bad things.

A bay on Jeju Island

Before You Watch

A Fill in the blanks. Use the words in the box.

tour guide   divers   seafood

In Korea, there is a group of woman _____. They go to the
sea every day to catch _____, like octopus and shellfish.
Some of the women are not divers. One of them works with tourists.
She is a _____.

While You Watch

A ▶ Watch the video. Circle **T** for *true* and **F** for *false*.

1. Diving is difficult and dangerous.   **T   F**
2. The water is cold.   **T   F**
3. The divers can stay underwater for
   ten minutes.   **T   F**

4. Sunny Hong is a diver.   **T   F**
5. The women sell the seafood.   **T   F**

After You Watch

A ⟳ Sunny Hong speaks English. She is a tour guide. She is not a diver.
She says, "I am lucky." How can speaking English help *you*?

Communication

A What jobs do women do well? What jobs do men do well? Make a list in your notebook.

B ⟳ Work with a partner. Compare your lists. Are they the same? Do you agree with your partner?

Work, Rest, and Play

Parents sleep in the gymnasium of Central China Normal University after accompanying their children to their first day of school.

Look at the photo, answer the questions:

1 Which word or phrase describes this photo?

2 Where do you work, rest, and play?

UNIT 2 GOALS

1. Talk about a typical day

2. Talk about free time

3. Describe a special celebration or festival

4. Describe daily life in different communities

brush your teeth
get up
eat breakfast
go to bed
take a shower
catch the bus
go to the movies
take a nap
watch TV
visit friends
start work
eat out

Vocabulary

A Label the pictures. Use phrases from the box.

a. _____

b. _____

c. _____

d. _____

e. _____

f. _____

g. _____

h. _____

i. _____

j. _____

k. _____

l. _____

B Circle the activities in exercise **A** that you do every day.

C Make a list of other activities you do every day. Share your list with the class.

D In your notebook, write the activities from **A** and **C** that you do, in the order that you do them.

E Describe your weekday routine to a partner. Use *first, next, then,* and *finally.*

First I get up, and **then** I take a shower and brush my teeth.

Grammar: Simple present tense

Simple present tense	
Statements	**Negative**
I/You **start** work at eight o'clock. Alison **catches** the bus at five thirty. We/They **go** to the movies every Saturday.	I/You **don't start** work at nine o'clock. Alison **doesn't catch** the bus at six thirty. We/They **don't go** to the movies every Friday.
Yes/No **questions**	**Short answers**
Do you **start** work at eight o'clock? **Does** Alison **catch** the bus at five thirty? **Do** we/they **go** to the movies every Saturday?	Yes, I **do**. No, I **don't**. Yes, she **does**. No, she **doesn't**. Yes, we/they **do**. No, we/they **don't**.

*We use the simple present tense to talk about habits and things that are always true.

A Complete the questions and answers.

1. **Q:** What time do you _____?

   A: I get up _____ seven o'clock.

2. **Q:** _____ you watch TV in the morning?

   A: No, I _____ watch TV in the morning.

3. **Q:** Do they _____ at ten o'clock?

   A: No, they _____ to bed at ten o'clock.

Prepositions of time		
on	**in**	**at**
on Saturday(s) on the 4th of July on Valentine's Day on the weekend	in the morning in the afternoon in the evening	at eight o'clock at night

Conversation

A 🔊 **7** Listen to the conversation. Does Mia work on Saturday?

Omar: So, Mia, you're <u>a secretary</u>.
Mia: That's right.
Omar: What time do you start work?
Mia: At <u>nine o'clock</u>.
Omar: Do you work on Saturday?
Mia: <u>Yes, I do, but we finish work at twelve o'clock on Saturdays</u>.
Omar: What do you do in the evenings?
Mia: <u>I watch TV or go to the movies</u>.

▲ Sara starts work at her job as a meteorologist at seven o'clock.

B 🔁 Practice the conversation with a partner. Switch roles and practice it again.

C 🔁 Change the underlined words and make a new conversation.

D 🔁 **GOAL CHECK** ✔ **Talk about a typical day**

Talk with your partner about what you do on Sundays. Mention the times you do each activity.

Listening

A 🔊 **8** Listen to the interview. What is Bob talking about? Circle the correct answer.

    a. his daily routine   **b.** his free time   **c.** his work

B 🔊 **8** Listen again. Circle the correct answer.

  1. On Sundays, Bob gets up at _____ .

    a. eight o'clock   **b.** nine o'clock   **c.** ten o'clock

  2. In the morning he _____ .

    a. takes a nap   **b.** visits friends   **c.** goes to a movie

  3. What does he do in the afternoon?

    a. He has lunch.   **b.** He watches sports on TV.   **c.** He visits friends.

  4. What does he do in the evening?

    a. He watches TV.   **b.** He goes out for dinner.   **c.** He visits friends.

Pronunciation: Verbs that end in -s

A 🔊 **9** Listen and check (✓) the correct column.

	Ends with /s/	Ends with /z/	Ends with /ɪz/
starts			
comes			
catches			
watches			
gets			
eats			
goes			

B 🔊 9 Listen again. Repeat the words.

C 🔁 Use the verbs from exercise **A** and write sentences. Have your partner read your sentences and check the pronunciation.

Communication

A Use the cues to write questions.

1. go to the movies / Saturdays *Do you go to the movies on Saturdays?*

2. get up / eight o'clock / the weekend _____

3. watch TV / Sunday mornings _____

4. take a nap / afternoon / weekend _____

5. eat out / weekend _____

B 👥 Interview two classmates. Use the questions in exercise **A**. Write *yes* or *no* in the chart.

Question	Classmate's name _____	Classmate's name _____
1.		
2.		
3.		
4.		
5.		

C 🔁 Tell a partner about the interviews.

> **Ana goes to the movies on Saturdays, and so does Sebastian.**

> **Ana goes to the movies on Saturdays, but Sebastian doesn't.**

> **Ana doesn't go to the movies on Saturdays, but Sebastian does.**

> **Ana doesn't go to the movies on Saturdays, and neither does Sebastian.**

D 🔁 | **GOAL CHECK** ✔ **Talk about free time**

Talk with a partner about your free time.

> **What do you do in your free time?**

Word Focus

We use *so do/does* to connect two affirmative sentences.

We use *neither do/does* to connect two negative sentences.

We use *but* when the sentences are different.

People in India enjoy Diwali, the Festival of Lights. They decorate streets and houses in many colors.

In the United States, Americans end their Independence Day celebrations with **fireworks**.

Language Expansion: Party words

A Read the text and captions. Pay attention to the words in **blue**.

All around the world, people need to **celebrate**. During the week we work, on weekends we rest, but we also need to have **fun**. **Festivals** are special celebrations. During festivals people dance, sing, wear different clothes, eat special food, and give **presents** to friends and family.

B Complete the sentences with the words in **blue**.

1. We watch the _____ on New Year's Eve.

2. I love parties. You can dance and sing. It's _____!

3. At Halloween, children wear _____ and _____ to cover their faces.

4. We _____ Christmas on the 24th and 25th of December.

5. I always give my mother _____ on her birthday.

6. I like to _____ the house for holidays.

C Discuss the following questions about your country with a partner.

1. Do you watch fireworks? If so, when?

2. Do you wear costumes? If so, when?

3. Do you give presents? If so, when?

In Venice, people wear **costumes** and cover their faces with **masks** to celebrate Carnival.

Grammar: Adverbs of frequency

0% _____ 100%

| never | sometimes | often | always |

Word order			
Subject	**Adverb of frequency**	**Verb**	
We	**always**	give	presents at Christmas.
We	**never**	dance	in the streets at Christmas.
Subject	***Be***	**Adverb of frequency**	
Christmas	is	**always**	in December.
Carnival	is	**usually**	in February or March.
*We use adverbs of frequency to say how often we do something.		*Adverbs of frequency come **before** the verb unless the verb is ***be.***	

A Unscramble the words to make sentences. Write the sentences.

1. always   We   have   a   on   Thanksgiving.   turkey   _____

2. Valentine's Day.   never   I   send   cards   on   _____

3. sometimes   on   visit   our   We   neighbors   New Year's.   _____

4. Nur   his   forgets   wife's   sometimes   birthday.   _____

5. is   in   summer.   It   hot   usually   _____

B Take turns. Tell a partner which sentences in exercise **A** are true for you.

Conversation

A 🔊 10 Listen to the conversation. Does Chuck have a family meal on New Year's Eve?

Diego: What do you do on New Year's Eve?

Chuck: Well, we sometimes go downtown. There are fireworks. It's really pretty. Other people invite friends to their house and they have a party.

Diego: Do you give presents to your friends and family?

Chuck: No, we never give presents on New Year's Eve.

Diego: Do you have a meal with your family?

Chuck: No, we do that on Christmas. On New Year's Eve we just have a party!

> **Real Language**
>
> We say we *party* when we have fun with family or friends.

B Practice the conversation with a partner. Switch roles and practice it again.

C Change the underlined words and make a new conversation.

D **GOAL CHECK** ✓ **Describe a special celebration or festival**

Talk with a partner about your favorite celebration or festival.

Reading

A 🔁 Look at the pictures. What kind of music does each show? Discuss with a partner.

B 🔁 In pairs, talk about your favorite types of music. When and where do you listen to music?

C Read the article. Choose the correct answer.

1. As a child, Eric Whitacre wanted to be _____ .

   a. a teacher   **c.** a composer
   b. in a band

2. When Eric Whitacre _____ for the first time, it surprised him.

   a. wrote music
   b. sang with a choir
   c. met a conductor

3. He became a famous conductor and _____ .

   a. composer   **c.** student
   b. singer

4. _____ makes it possible for people all over the world to join Eric Whitacre's virtual choir.

   a. Pop music   **c.** The Internet
   b. College

5. The people in the choir are united by _____ .

   a. a love of singing   **c.** family
   b. living near each other

WORD BANK

choir group of people that sing together
choral related to a choir
composer person who writes music
conductor person who leads a choir
virtual on computers or on the Internet

TED Ideas worth spreading

Eric Whitacre Composer/Conductor

A VIRTUAL CHOIR 2,000 VOICES STRONG

The following article is about Eric Whitacre. After Unit 3, you'll have the opportunity to watch some of Whitacre's TED Talk and learn more about his idea worth spreading.

Eric Whitacre is a **composer** and **conductor.** He is excited about using **choral** music to join people together from all around the world.

As a child, Eric Whitacre lived in a small town with many farms. He loved music. He didn't know how to read music, but he often played instruments. He always wanted to be part of a rock or pop band. Years later, he went to college. There he met the conductor of the college's **choir.** At first, Eric didn't want to join the choir, but finally he did.

The first time that Eric Whitacre sang with the choir, it was a big surprise. He thought that choral music was beautiful and interesting. He learned how to read music, and then he began to write musical pieces. He became a successful composer and conductor.

Whitacre's choir is very unusual because it's completely **virtual.** The Internet makes this possible. The members of the choir don't know each other. They are different ages, from different countries, and have different professions. But they are united by their love of singing and their desire to be part of a worldwide community that makes beautiful music.

" The most transformative experience I've ever had . . . I felt for the first time in my life that I was part of something bigger than myself. "

– Eric Whitacre

A choir blends many voices together to make music.

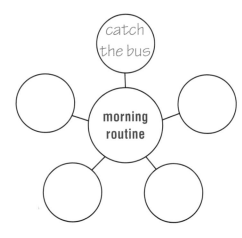

The virtual choir enables people who begin their daily routines at very different times to come together and make music. At 8 a.m. in the United States, Melody is waking up. What time is it for Georgie and Cheryl Ang? What do you think they are doing?

Writing

A Complete the paragraph about a singer's morning routine.

In the morning, I _____ early, around 6:30. Next to my room is the bathroom, where I _____. Then, I _____ in the kitchen. I never watch TV at breakfast; I often _____ to music.

B Fill in the word web with activities that are related to morning routines.

C 🔁 Make a word web about your daily routine. Then write a paragraph describing your day. With a partner, talk about how the singer's lifestyle is the same or different than yours.

Communication

A 🔁 Eric Whitacre always spent a lot of his free time making music. Now he's a famous composer and conductor. With a partner, talk about the following: What do you love to do in your free time? What is your dream job? Are they related?

B 🔁 **GOAL CHECK** ✓ Describe daily life in different communities

Read the paragraph on the left. Pick a singer from the virtual choir. Imagine his or her daily routine. With a partner, write a paragraph describing the day. Talk about how the singer's lifestyle is the same or different than yours.

Georgie from England   **Cheryl Ang from Singapore**   **Melody Myers from the U.S.**

Monkeys in Lopburi

Before You Watch

A You are going to watch a video about a monkey festival. Circle five words or expressions you think you will hear in the video.

food	take a nap
dance	watch TV
visit friends	water
presents	tourist

While You Watch

A ▶ Watch the video. Circle **T** for *true* or **F** for *false*.

1. The monkey festival is on the last Sunday in November.   **T   F**

2. The monkeys dance.   **T   F**

3. The people give the monkeys lots of food.   **T   F**

4. The monkeys cut the electric and telephone cables.   **T   F**

B ▶ Watch the video again and answer the questions.

1. In which country is Lopburi?

2. What do the people do for the monkey festival?

3. What is the first goal of the festival?

4. What is the second goal of the festival?

After You Watch

The monkeys of Lopburi are interesting because in other countries, monkeys don't live with people. They are **wild**. But in Lopburi, they live with people. They are **tame.**

A Write the animals from the box in the correct column. Add other animals.

birds cats cows
lions horses elephants

Wild	Tame

Going Places

Hot air balloons fill the sky above the Cappadocia region of Turkey.

UNIT 3 GOALS

1. Identify possessions

2. Ask for and give personal travel information

3. Give travel advice

4. Share special travel tips with others

Vocabulary

A In what order do you do these things when you travel? Number the pictures.

▲ take a taxi

▲ buy your ticket

▲ board the airplane

▲ go through security

▲ claim your baggage

▲ go through immigration

▲ go through customs

▲ check in

▲ buy duty-free goods

▲ pack your bags

B Complete the sentences. Use a phrase from exercise **A.**

1. After you _____ , you can leave the airport.

2. Do I have to take off my shoes when I _____?

3. At the airport, the first thing you do is _____ .

4. Many people _____ like perfume and chocolates at the airport.

5. When you _____ , you can only take a small bag.

6. Make sure you don't take the wrong bag when you

   _____ at the carousel.

C What do you do when you are waiting for a plane? What do you do on the plane? Use a dictionary or ask your teacher for help. Share your ideas with the class.

Grammar: Possession

Possessive adjective	Possessive pronoun	*Belong to*	
my	mine		me.
your	yours		you.
his	his	It **belongs to**	him.
her	hers	They **belong to**	her.
our	ours		us.
their	theirs		them.

Real Language

To ask about possession, we can say *Whose _____ is this?*

A Complete the conversations. Use a word or phrase for possession.

1. **A:** Excuse me, is this _____ bag? **B:** No, it's not _____ .

2. **A:** Is this Anna's bag? **B:** No, _____ is green.

3. **A:** _____ ticket is this? **B:** I think it _____ Shawn.

B Answer the questions using *belong to* and a possessive pronoun.

1. Whose passport is this? (Ali) *It belongs to Ali. It's his.* _____

2. Whose keys are these? (my keys) _____

3. Whose camera is this? (my sister's) _____

4. Whose bags are these? (John and Lucy's) _____

5. Whose tickets are these? (Logan's and mine) _____

Conversation

A 🔊 **11** Listen to the conversation. Who does the bag belong to?

Anna:	Whose <u>bag</u> is this?
Bill:	It's not mine.
Anna:	Maybe it's Jim's. Is this your <u>bag</u>, Jim?
Jim:	No, mine is <u>black</u>.
Anna:	Well, whose is it?
Bill:	Maybe it belongs to this woman. Excuse me, does this <u>bag</u> belong to you?
Woman:	Yes, it's mine. Thank you so much.

B Practice the conversation in a group of four students. Switch roles and practice it again.

C Change the underlined words and make a new conversation.

D **GOAL CHECK** ✓ **Identify possessions**

Give a personal item, like your pen or watch, to the teacher. The teacher will then give you someone else's personal item. You have to find the owner.

Do you know whose watch this is?

Does this watch belong to you?

Is this your watch?

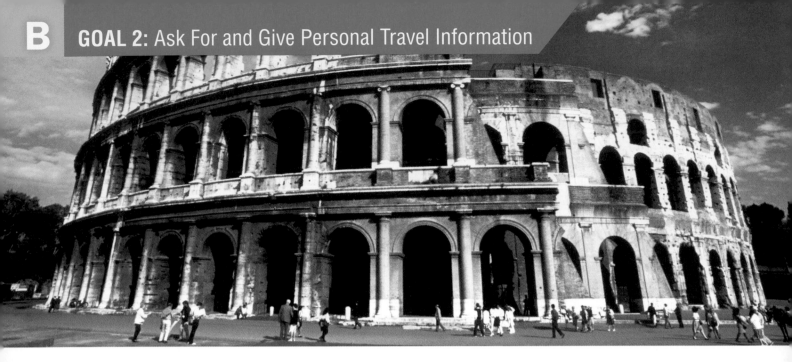

B GOAL 2: Ask For and Give Personal Travel Information

▲ Rome is one of the most popular places to travel to in the world.

Listening

A 🔊 **12** Listen to the conversations. Where do the conversations take place?

Conversation 1 _____   **a.** hotel reception

Conversation 2 _____   **b.** immigration

Conversation 3 _____   **c.** check-in counter

B 🔊 **12** Listen again. Circle **T** for *true* and **F** for *false*.

Conversation 1

1. The man books a window seat.   T   F

2. The man has two bags.   T   F

Conversation 2

1. This is the woman's first visit to the United States.   T   F

2. The woman is staying in the United States for three weeks. T   F

Conversation 3

1. The man is staying at the hotel for one night.   T   F

2. The man has one bag.   T   F

Pronunciation: Rising intonation on lists

A 🔊 **13** Listen and repeat the sentences.

1. I'm going to London, Paris, Rome, and Madrid.

2. I'll be in Rome on June 21st, 22nd, and 23rd.

3. In Rome, I want to visit the Colosseum, the Vatican, and the Spanish Steps.

4. To get around, I can take the metro, a taxi, or a Vespa.

one	first	1st
two	second	2nd
three	third	3rd
four	fourth	4th
five	fifth	5th
ten	tenth	10th
twenty	twentieth	20th
thirty-one	thirty-first	31st

B 🔁 Practice these sentences with a partner.

1. When we are in Peru, we are going to visit Lima, Cusco, and Machu Picchu.
2. We'll be in Cusco on the 4th, 5th, and 6th of October.
3. To get from Cusco to Machu Picchu, you can take a train, bus, or taxi.
4. The taxi is quick, clean, and expensive.

> What is your first name?

> My first name is Wahid.

Communication

A 🔁 Take turns. Ask a partner questions to fill out the immigration form below with his or her information.

Department of Immigration **PERMISSION TO ENTER**	
1. First name	8. Principal destination in this country
2. Middle name	
3. Family name	9. Hotel and/or street address
4. Date of birth	
5. Place of birth	10. Entry date
6. Nationality	11. Departure date
7. Country of residence	12. Reason for visit
FORM 12a/PTO (Revised08) [Pursuant to Section 211(d)(3) of the IPA]	

B 🔁 **GOAL CHECK** ✔ **Ask for and give personal travel information**

Work with a new partner. Tell your new partner about your previous partner, using the information on the form in exercise **A**.

> His destination is . . .

▲ Children in the Plaza de Armas, Cusco, Peru

▲ travel insurance

▲ international driver's license

▲ visa

▲ credit cards

▲ passport

Language Expansion: Travel documents and money

A Complete the sentences. Use the names of the travel documents.

1. You need a(n) _____ to drive a car in a foreign country.

2. In some countries, you need a(n) _____ to enter.

3. It's a good idea to buy _____. Medical bills are expensive.

4. Your _____ is your photo ID in any foreign country.

5. You can buy a(n) _____ on the Internet. But you need to write down or print the confirmation number.

B 🔁 Talk to a partner. What is the best form of money to take on your trip? Why?

Give an opinion

> I think credit cards are good.

> The best idea is to take . . .

Give a reason

> People steal . . .

> . . . don't accept . . .

> People lose cash.

▲ airline ticket

▲ cash

C 🔁 Your father is planning a vacation. He usually uses a travel agent. You think he should do the planning online.

1. Write a list of the things he can get online, for example, hotel reservations and museum tickets.

2. With a partner, role-play persuading your father to buy online.

> You should book a hotel online because it is cheaper.

> No, you should ask a travel agent, so you know the hotel is safe.

Grammar: *Should* for advice

Should				
Subject	*Should*	Adverb of frequency	Verb	Complement
You	**should**	(always)	make	a copy of your passport.
You	**shouldn't**		wear	expensive jewelry.

*We use *should/shouldn't* to give advice.

Questions with *should*			
Should	Subject	Verb	Complement
Should	I	take	a taxi from the airport?

*We use questions with *should* to ask for advice.

A Ask for advice. Read the responses and write the questions.

1. **Q:** Should I take the shuttle bus to the airport?

   A: Yes, you should. The shuttle bus is quick and cheap.

2. **Q:** _____

   A: No, you shouldn't. It is hot at the beach. You don't need a sweater.

3. **Q:** _____

   A: Yes, you should. Credit cards are accepted in a lot of shops.

4. **Q:** _____

   A: No, you shouldn't. It's dangerous to carry cash.

B Ask the questions in exercise **A** and give different advice. Take turns with a partner.

Conversation

A 🔊 14 Listen to the conversation. What does Claudia want from the United States?

Ayumi: Hi, Claudia. You know the USA. Can you give me some advice? I'm going to New York in January.

Claudia: Lucky you! How can I help?

Ayumi: First: Should I buy travel insurance?

Claudia: Yes, you should. Hospitals and doctors are very expensive in the U.S.

Ayumi: OK. That's another $200. What about clothes? What should I take?

Claudia: You should take a warm sweater and some gloves and a scarf.

Ayumi: Hmm, that's another $100.

Claudia: Oh, just one more thing! Don't forget to buy me a nice present, like a new watch.

Ayumi: Oh no! That's another $500! Traveling is expensive!

B Practice the conversation with a partner. Switch roles and practice it again.

C Change the underlined words and make a new conversation.

D **GOAL CHECK** ✔ **Give travel advice**

Discuss travel tips for visitors to your country. Think about the following topics.

- transportation
- how to carry money
- Can you drink the water?

▲ Washington Square Park, New York City

Reading

A Read the article. Then answer the questions.

1. Do you think the author enjoys traveling? _____ _____

2. Why should you check the expiration date of your passport? _____ _____

3. Why should you tie a sock to your bag? _____ _____

4. Why should you take a good book when you travel? _____ _____

B Circle **T** for *true* and **F** for *false*.

1. You need a lot of documents to travel.   **T** **F**

2. You need to take a lot of clothes in your bag.   **T** **F**

3. Bags can be hard to identify at the airport.   **T** **F**

4. Flights are never late.   **T** **F**

5. Airplane food is always good.   **T** **F**

Word Focus

expiration date = the date a thing comes to an end or can no longer be used

Real Language

We use the expression *share some pointers* to say *give advice*.

SMART

TRAVELER

EXPERT OPINION

In his book Easy Travel, *Mike Connelly **shares some pointers** on making travel easy:*

DOCUMENTS Make sure you have all your documents: passport, visas, tickets, etc. You should always check the **expiration date** of your passport. Many countries won't let you enter with less than six months left on your passport. Don't forget to buy travel insurance. Medical bills can be very expensive, especially in the United States and Europe. Finally, you should make copies of all your important documents and credit cards and keep them in another bag.

PACKING My advice is—always travel light! I hate to carry heavy bags. Just take the minimum. There is an old saying: *Breakfast in Berlin. Dinner in Delhi. Bags in Bangkok!* So, don't pack anything important in your check-in bag; put important things in your carry-on bag. You don't want to arrive home without your house keys. Another tip—don't use expensive suitcases. People don't steal dirty old bags. Finally, here's a good little tip—tie a sock or brightly colored string to your bag. Why? So you can quickly see your bag on the airport carousel.

THE AIRPORT My first piece of advice is that you should always carry a good book. It helps to pass the time as you wait for your delayed flight. Don't forget to take a sweater or a jacket on the plane. It can get cold on a long night flight. And then there is airline food. Take a snack (cookies or fruit) with you. Sometimes the food is late, sometimes it doesn't arrive at all, and it's never very good.

▲ Riviera Maya, Mexico

Communication

A 🔁 You have won a vacation for two people and you can choose where to go. Choose one of the following and be ready to say why you chose it.

Resort in Mexico   Historical tour of Angkor Wat, Cambodia

World Cup in Brazil   Adventure tourism in New Zealand

Trekking in the Himalayas

> Do you think we should take . . . ?

> I think we should take . . . because . . .

> I don't think we should take . . . because . . .

B 🔁 Read the list below—your teacher will help you. You can only take five of these items. Discuss which items to take with a partner. Give your reasons.

1. sun block
2. binoculars
3. warm clothes
4. first-aid kit
5. international driver's license
6. water sterilization tablets
7. umbrella

8. maps
9. money belt
10. guidebook
11. sunglasses
12. hair dryer
13. penknife
14. smartphone

Writing

A Write travel tips for your vacation in your notebook.

B 🔗 **GOAL CHECK** ✓ **Share special travel tips with others**

Read your travel tips to a partner. Then share them with the class.

Before You Watch

A Do you have working dogs in your country? How do these dogs help people?

While You Watch

A ▶ Watch the video. Circle the names of things you see.

uniform　　apples　　suitcase　　passport　　mango　　beef jerky

B ▶ Watch the video again. Circle **T** for *true* and **F** for *false*.

1. Brent and Stockton play before they start work.　　**T**　**F**
2. Detector dogs look for meat.　　**T**　**F**
3. Stockton does not find the meat.　　**T**　**F**
4. Stockton eats the meat he finds.　　**T**　**F**
5. Stockton is learning slowly.　　**T**　**F**

Word Focus

disease　to bother　illegal

Rats are dirty. Sometimes they carry **disease.**

Hey, kids! Please be quiet. I'm trying to work. You're **bothering** me.

You can't park your car there. It's not allowed. It's **illegal.**

After You Watch/Communication

A 🔗 In the video, we saw that dogs can be very useful in airports. Work with a partner to write a list of possible problems with dogs in airports.

B 🔗 With a partner, role-play the following situations.

In **Situation 1,** Student A is a dog handler, and Student B is a passenger. The dog is sniffing in Student B's bag, and Student B does not like dogs.

In **Situation 2,** Student A is a passenger that has fruit in his or her bag. The fruit is a gift. Student B is the dog handler and has to take the fruit.

TEDTALKS

Before You Watch

A Write the correct word under each picture.

| singer | conductor | choir | piano |

1. _____

2. _____

3. _____

4. _____

B 🔄 Work with a partner. Try to think of one example each for items 1–4 in exercise **A**. Share your answers with the class.

C Complete the sentences using the words from the box.

> **community** group of similar people
> **connection** relationship
> **post** put information up
> **record** store music so it can be listened to later
> **virtual** on a computer

1. The sisters had a very strong _____.

2. Please _____ your music for him.

3. People who live in a neighborhood are part of the _____.

4. The video game had a _____ world that players could play in.

5. I will _____ this information on the Web site for my classmates.

> Eric Whitacre's idea worth spreading is that technology and music can connect us in wonderful, unexpected ways. Watch Whitacre's full TED Talk on TED.com.

D You are going to watch a TED Talk about a virtual choir. What do you think you will see in the video? What things do you think a person should do if they are going to start an online community? Discuss them with a partner.

> **You should have a computer.**

While You Watch

A ▶ Look at the pictures and quotes on the next page. Then watch the TED Talk. As you watch, put the pictures in order. Write the number in the box under the picture.

B ▶ Watch the TED Talk again. Complete the sentences using the words from the box.

| connect | singers | Malta |
| Sleep | Britlin | Jordan |

1. A girl named _____ posted a video for Eric Whitacre. Her video gave Eric the idea for the first virtual choir.

2. Eric created a virtual choir to _____ people around the world.

3. The second virtual choir had 2,051 _____.

4. The second virtual choir had singers from many countries, such as _____ and _____.

5. Eric Whitacre chose a piece called _____ for the second virtual choir.

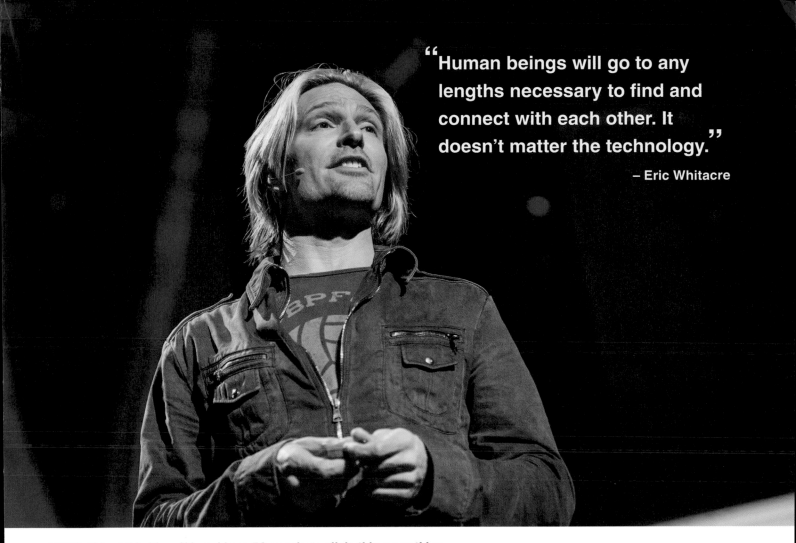

> " **Human beings will go to any lengths necessary to find and connect with each other. It doesn't matter the technology.** "

– Eric Whitacre

"I had this idea: if I could get 50 people to all do this same thing, sing their parts—soprano, alto, tenor, and bass—wherever they were in the world, post their videos to YouTube, we could cut it all together and create a virtual choir."

"I just couldn't believe the poetry of all of it—these souls all on their own desert island, sending electronic messages in bottles to each other."

"For Virtual Choir 2.0 . . . our final tally was 2,051 videos from 58 different countries. From Malta, Madagascar, Thailand, Vietnam, Jordan, Egypt, Israel, as far north as Alaska, and as far south as New Zealand."

"I posted a conductor track of myself conducting. And it's in complete silence when I filmed it, because I was only hearing the music in my head, imagining the choir that would one day come to be."

Virtual Choir 2.0

After You Watch

A Read the sentences. Correct the false information.

1. A choir has to use the Internet._____*virtual choir*_____

2. In Eric Whitacre's virtual choir, all the singers record their videos at the same time._____

3. In their testimonials, the singers said that being in the virtual choir did not make them feel connected to other people around the world.

_____

4. All of the members of the choir are now good friends, even though they live in different countries and do not meet in person.

_____

B Most conductors work with singers in person, but Eric Whitacre conducts a choir online. With a group, take turns naming occupations. For each one, discuss whether it is possible for people in the occupation to work in a virtual way.

Teacher
- Teachers usually work in person.
- It is also possible for them to work in a virtual way. Teachers can teach online.

C Someone you know wants to be part of Eric Whitacre's next virtual choir. What advice would you give? With a partner, brainstorm a list of verbs (*be, learn, post,* etc.). Use *should/shouldn't* and the verbs to write five pieces of advice in your notebook.

Rural Alaska

D One woman in the virtual choir lives in rural Alaska, 400 miles from the nearest town. What do you think her life is like? Why is the choir important to her? How do music and technology connect her with people around the world? Discuss with a partner.

E Do you like to do the following things online, in person, or both? Add your own idea. Then answer by placing a check (✓) in the appropriate box. Then interview your classmates about what they prefer. Write each classmate's initials in the appropriate box. Share with the class.

	Virtual world	In person	Both
1. play games			
2. take classes			
3. talk to family			
4. shop			
5. explore the world			
6. _____			

F Pick one of the activities in exercise **E.** Write a short paragraph about why you think it is better to do that activity online or in person. Use some of the words provided.

to live nearby/far away	to connect	to spend time together/alone
to feel lonely/alone	to meet	

Challenge! What other virtual choirs has Eric Whitacre conducted? Visit TED.com to find out. Then share what you learned with a group. Be sure to include the name of the musical piece, the number of singers, the number of countries, and a short description of the piece. Use at least two descriptive adjectives.

Food

A colorful blend of spices is displayed in a variety of measuring spoons. People around the world use spices to flavor and preserve food.

UNIT 4 GOALS

1. Give a recipe

2. Order a meal

3. Talk about diets

4. Discuss unusual foods

drinks   dairy products
vegetables   fruit
protein   meat

Vocabulary

A 🗨 Talk to a partner. Choose a word or phrase from the box to describe each group of foods.

> **Juice and water are drinks.**

cheese
butter
milk
juice
soda
coffee
tea
water
lemons
banana
oranges
apples
peppers
tomatoes
onions
lettuce
potatoes
chicken
eggs
fish
shrimp
turkey bacon
sausages
steak

B 🗨 With your partner, think of some other foods you know and write them in the correct group. Then share them with the class.

Grammar: *Some* and *any* with count and non-count nouns

Count and non-count nouns	
Singular	**Plural**
This is a lemon.	Those are lemons.
This is milk.	~~Those are milks.~~
*For nouns you can count, we add -s or -es to form the plural. *Nouns you cannot count don't have a plural form.	

Some and *any*	Count nouns		Non-count nouns
	Singular	**Plural**	
Statement	We need an apple.	There are **some** oranges on the table.	There is **some** cheese on the table.
Negative	We don't have a lemon.	There aren't **any** bananas at the store.	We don't have **any** milk.
Question	Do we have a red pepper?	Are there **any** eggs?	Do you have **any** butter?

*You can also use *some* for questions with *could*.
 *Could I have **some** milk?*

A In your notebook, write the food words from the picture in two columns: *Count nouns* and *Non-count nouns*.

B 🔀 Add other food words to the chart. Use a dictionary if necessary. Share your words with your group.

C Complete the sentences with *some* or *any*.

1. Do we have _____ tomatoes?

2. Pass me _____ apples, please.

3. There isn't _____ milk in the fridge.

4. I think there is _____ cheese on the table.

5. There aren't _____ eggs.

6. Could I have _____ water, please?

Conversation

A 🔊 **15** Listen to the conversation. What do you need to make a Spanish omelet?

Lee: Let's make a Spanish omelet.
Diana: Great. What do we need?
Lee: OK. It says here you need some olive oil. Do we have any olive oil?
Diana: No, we don't, but it doesn't matter; we have some corn oil. That will do.
Lee: Next, we need some potatoes, a large onion, and a red pepper.
Diana: We don't have a red pepper.
Lee: Never mind. We can use a green pepper.
Diana: OK. And then we need some eggs. Four eggs.
Lee: OK! Let's begin!

B 🔀 Practice the conversation with a partner. Switch roles and practice it again.

C 🔀 Choose a new recipe and repeat the conversation.

Real Language

We can use *never mind* or *it doesn't matter* to show something is not important.

Word Focus

Names of fractions:
$\frac{1}{2}$ = one-half
$\frac{1}{3}$ = one-third
$\frac{1}{4}$ = one-fourth or one-quarter

Spanish omelet
Ingredients
1/2 cup of olive oil
5 potatoes
1 large onion
1 red pepper
4 eggs
salt and pepper

Quiche from France
Ingredients
3 eggs
2 cups of grated cheese
2 cups of milk
2 onions
salt and pepper

Frittata from Italy
Ingredients
1/4 cup of butter
3 or 4 eggs
1/2 cup of cheese
3 ounces of turkey bacon
2 tomatoes
salt and pepper

Quick Egg Dishes
from Around the world

D 🔀 **GOAL CHECK** ✔ **Give a recipe**

Tell a partner the name of a dish you like. Explain the recipe by describing the ingredients you need to prepare it.

▲ A busy restaurant in Guilin, China

Listening

A 🔊 16 Listen to the **waiter** taking an order from **customers.** How many customers are there?

B 🔊 16 Listen again and write the food and drink that each person ordered.

	Drink	Food
Man		
Woman		

Word Focus

waiter = A *waiter* is a person who works in a restaurant and serves food and drinks.

customer = A *customer* is a person who buys goods or services.

Menu

Appetizers

Chicken 'n Cheese
Deep-fried chicken served with fresh tomatoes and sliced Cheddar cheese

Vegetable Soup
Made from fresh vegetables

Main Dishes

Seashore Shrimp
Grilled shrimp served with peppers and boiled rice

Butter-Baked Chicken
Roasted half-chicken in a lemon sauce served with carrots and potatoes

Filet Mignon
8 oz. grilled tenderloin steak, served with iceberg lettuce and your favorite salad dressing

Drinks
Mineral water, iced tea, coffee

C 🔊 16 Listen again. Who asked these questions?

1. Are you ready to order? _waiter_ _____

2. Do you have any mineral water? _____

3. What would you recommend? _____

4. Does the filet mignon come with salad? _____

5. Anything else? _____

Pronunciation: Reduced forms *Do you have . . .* and *Would you like . . .*

A 🔊 17 Listen to the full form and the reduced form.

B 🔊 18 Listen and check (✓) the correct column. Then listen again and repeat.

	Full form	Reduced form
1. Do you have a pen?		
2. Would you like some more bread?		
3. Do you have any paper?		
4. Would you like some coffee?		
5. Do you have any change?		

Communication

A 🔁 With a partner, role-play the following situation.

Student A You work in a supermarket. Serve the customer.

Student B You want to make one of the egg dishes on page 45. Ask for the food you need from the sales assistant.

B 🔁 **GOAL CHECK** ✓ **Order a meal**

Work with a partner. Choose roles and role-play. Switch roles and role-play again.

Student A You are a customer in a restaurant. Order a meal from the menu on page 46.

Student B You are the waiter. Take the customer's order.

▲ broccoli

▲ cauliflower

▲ beans

▲ whole-wheat bagel

▲ breakfast cereal

▲ nuts

Language Expansion: Diets

Many people eat a special diet. Sometimes, people go on a diet to lose weight and sometimes so that they will feel healthier. Here are two diets: a high-fiber diet and a high-protein diet. The first has a lot of food that contains fiber, for example, whole wheat, brown rice, and maize. The second has a lot of food that contains protein, like meat, fish, and cheese.

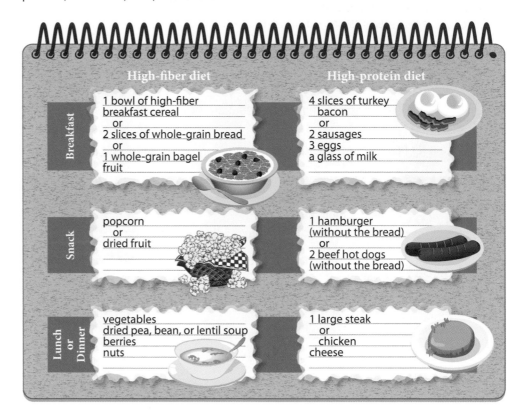

	High-fiber diet	High-protein diet
Breakfast	1 bowl of high-fiber breakfast cereal or 2 slices of whole-grain bread or 1 whole-grain bagel fruit	4 slices of turkey bacon or 2 sausages 3 eggs a glass of milk
Snack	popcorn or dried fruit	1 hamburger (without the bread) or 2 beef hot dogs (without the bread)
Lunch or Dinner	vegetables dried pea, bean, or lentil soup berries nuts	1 large steak or chicken cheese

A Write the names of the foods on the page in the correct column.

High-fiber diet	High-protein diet

▲ hamburger

▲ tuna salad

B Add the names of other high-fiber and high-protein foods you know to the chart.

Grammar: *How much* and *How many* with quantifiers: *lots of, a few, a little*

	Information question	Quantifiers	
		++++	**+**
Count	**How many** oranges do you need?	I need **lots of** oranges.	I need **a few** oranges.
Non-count	**How much** milk do we have?	We have **lots of** milk.	We have **a little** milk.

*We use *lots of* and *a few* to answers questions about quantity.
*We use *a little* to answer questions about small quantities we cannot count.

A Complete the sentences using *a little* or *a few*.

1. There is only _____ tuna salad in the fridge.

2. We only need _____ apples.

3. Please bring _____ bananas.

4. I only take _____ sugar in my coffee.

5. There are just _____ peppers left.

B Fill in the blanks with *How much, How many, lots of, a few,* or *a little*.

1. Q: ___How many___ potatoes would you like?   **A:** Just ___a few___, thanks.

2. Q: _____ steak do we need?   **A:** There are eight of us, so we need _____ steak.

3. Q: _____ broccoli would you like?   **A:** I'm not very hungry. Just _____.

4. Q: _____ apples do we need?   **A:** About 20. We eat _____ apples.

C With a partner, use the words in exercise **A** on page 48 to ask and answer questions.

Conversation

A 19 Listen to the conversation. Can Pat eat popcorn?

How much cauliflower would you like?

Just a little.

Kim: You're looking good.
Pat: Thanks, Kim. I'm on a special diet. It's a high-fiber diet.
Kim: High fiber? You mean lots of bread and fruit?
Pat: That's right.
Kim: How much bread can you eat for breakfast?
Pat: I can eat two slices of whole-grain bread for breakfast or one bowl of high-fiber cereal.
Kim: And what about snacks?
Pat: No problem. I can eat lots of popcorn and dried fruit.
Kim: Mmm, sounds like a delicious diet. Maybe I'll join you.

B Practice the conversation with a partner. Switch roles and practice it again.

C Make a new conversation for the high-protein diet.

D **GOAL CHECK** ✔ **Talk about diets**

With a partner, have a conversation about your own diet or another diet you know.

Reading

A Look at the photos. Do people eat insects in your country?

B Read the article. Answer the questions.

1. What insects are on the menu in the restaurant? _____

2. In Thailand, are insects luxury food? _____

3. How many bits of insects are allowed in peanut butter? _____

4. What does the author order? _____

5. Do you like to eat insects? Give your reasons. _____
_____
_____
_____

▲ Crickets, grasshoppers, and other insects-on-a-stick are for sale at a Donghaumen Night Market near Wangfujing Dongcheng, Beijing, China.

Word Focus

luxury = A *luxury* is something we do not really need.

unintentionally = When something happens *unintentionally*, we don't mean for it to happen.

New York City, USA

BUGS AS FOOD

I am sitting in an expensive New York restaurant, and I read the menu. I can't believe my eyes! Chocolate-covered crickets. Wow! I can also order Ant Egg Soup or Silkworm Fried Rice. And it's expensive—$25 for 5 crickets!

I don't like the idea of eating insects. However, in many countries insects are not **luxury** food. They are part of an everyday diet. In Thailand, open-air markets sell silkworms and grasshoppers. Movie theaters in South America sell roasted ants as snacks instead of popcorn.

I am probably eating insects without knowing it, anyway. "It's estimated that the average human eats half a kilogram (1.1 pounds) of insects each year, **unintentionally,**" says Lisa Monachelli, director of youth and family programs at New Canaan Nature Center in Connecticut. "For example, in the United States, chocolate can have up to 60 bits of bugs (like legs and heads) per 100 grams. Tomato sauce can contain 30 fly eggs per 100 grams, and peanut butter can have 30 insect bits per 100 grams."

Well, if I am eating insects anyway . . . I decide to order the chocolate-covered crickets, and hey, they taste good.

People eat bugs for food all over the world.

rattlesnake

Communication

Many countries have unusual food. At least, it is unusual to visitors to the country. To the people of the country, it is not unusual. In fact, it is often special food—a delicacy. Here are some examples. Do you eat any of these in your country?

Texas, USA	**Rattlesnake**
Mexico	**Ceviche—uncooked fish**
China	**Bird's nest soup**
Scotland	**Haggis—sheep's stomach**
France	**Frog's legs**
Saudi Arabia	**Sheep's eyeballs**

A Write the delicacies in the chart.

> **I would never eat haggis.**

I would **definitely** eat this. ☺	I **might** eat this. 😐	I would **never** eat this. ☹

Fried Rattlesnake

1. Catch and kill a rattlesnake.
2. Remove the skin and intestines.
3. Cut it into 5-cm pieces.
4. Fry it in very hot oil.
5. Eat it!

B Read your answers from the chart to your partner.

C | **GOAL CHECK** ✔ **Discuss unusual foods**

Make a list of delicacies that visitors to your country might find unusual. Share it with the class. Answer questions from the class.

Writing

A Write a recipe for one of the delicacies in exercise **C**.

whale shark

▲ great white shark

Before You Watch

A 🔁 Work with a partner. Discuss these questions.

1. Which of these fish can kill you?   2. How can they kill you?

While You Watch

A ▶ Watch the video. Circle **T** for *true* and **F** for *false*.

1. The pufferfish is not expensive.   **T**   **F**

2. Chef Hayashi has a license to prepare *fugu*.   **T**   **F**

3. About 30 people die every year because they eat *fugu*.   **T**   **F**

4. American General Douglas MacArthur introduced a test
   for *fugu* chefs.   **T**   **F**

5. Tom likes the *fugu*.   **T**   **F**

▲ stingray

B Answer the questions.

1. Is Tom worried about eating *fugu*? _____

2. When did Chef Hayashi get his license? _____

3. How does *fugu* poison kill a person? _____

4. How many people can a tiger *fugu* kill? _____

▲ stonefish

After You Watch

A 🔁 Discuss these questions with a partner.

1. Why do you think people like to eat *fugu*?

2. Would you eat *fugu*?

▲ pufferfish

British climber Hazel Findlay climbs a sea cliff in Maine, USA.

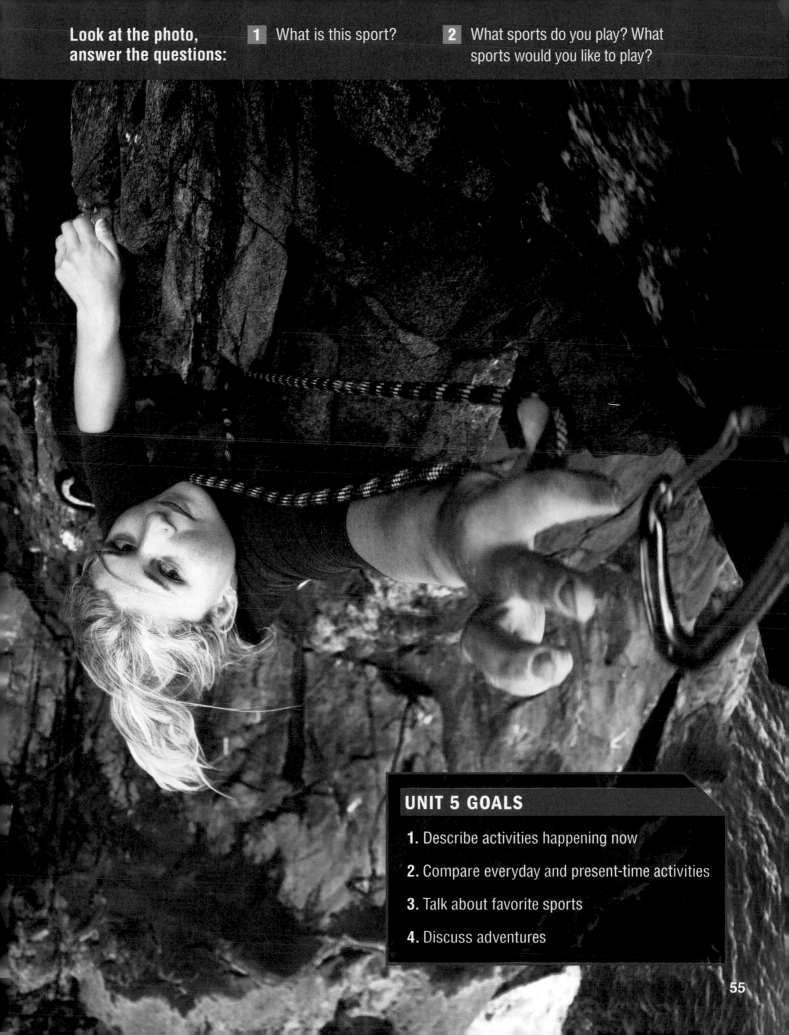

Look at the photo, answer the questions:

1 What is this sport?

2 What sports do you play? What sports would you like to play?

UNIT 5 GOALS

1. Describe activities happening now

2. Compare everyday and present-time activities

3. Talk about favorite sports

4. Discuss adventures

1. _____

Vocabulary

A Read the conversations. Use the words in blue to label the photos.

Anna is studying for a test. She is bored and tired, so she is calling some friends.

Anna:	Hi! What's up? What are you doing?
Bridget:	We're at the beach. Kenny's swimming and the others are playing soccer. How about you? What are you doing?
Anna:	I'm studying! Grrrr!

2. _____

Anna:	Hi Jill. What are you doing?
Jill:	I'm at Eagle Rocks with Antonia and Pete. They're climbing and I'm hiking. It's really cool. Why don't you come?
Anna:	I can't. I'm studying for a test.

Anna:	Hi Leyla. What's happening?
Leyla:	Hi. I'm at the gym. I'm taking a break. Mary and Catalina are here, too. Mary is lifting weights and Catalina is jogging. What are you doing?
Anna:	I'm studying. Boring!!!

3. _____

6. _____   7. _____

4. _____

B 🔁 Take turns. Read the clues to a partner. Guess an activity from exercise **A**. Write your answer.

1. You do this in the gym. _____

2. You do this in a swimming pool. _____

3. You play this with a ball. _____

4. It is like running. _____

5. You do this in the mountains. _____

5. _____

6. You do this when you are tired. _____

Grammar: Present continuous tense

	Present continuous tense	
Statement	I **am playing** soccer	right now.
Negative	They **are not taking** a break	at the moment.
		now.
Yes/No question	**Are** you **studying**	right now?
		at the moment?
Wh- question	What **are** you **doing**	now?

*We use the present continuous tense to talk about things that are happening at the moment.

A Complete the message. Use the present continuous tense of the verbs given.

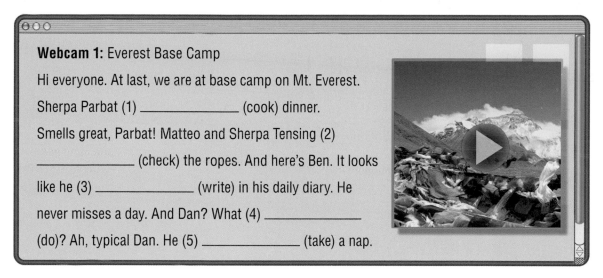

Webcam 1: Everest Base Camp

Hi everyone. At last, we are at base camp on Mt. Everest.

Sherpa Parbat (1) _____ (cook) dinner.

Smells great, Parbat! Matteo and Sherpa Tensing (2)

_____ (check) the ropes. And here's Ben. It looks

like he (3) _____ (write) in his daily diary. He

never misses a day. And Dan? What (4) _____

(do)? Ah, typical Dan. He (5) _____ (take) a nap.

Conversation

A 🔊 **20** Listen to the conversation. What are the twins doing?

Mom:	Hey, it's quiet today. Where are the kids?
Dad:	Well, Mario's playing basketball in the yard.
Mom:	What's Carla doing?
Dad:	She's swimming in the pool.
Mom:	And the twins? What are they doing?
Dad:	Uhh . . . I don't know.
Mom:	Hey, you two! What are you doing?
Twins:	We're playing soccer!

B 🔁 Practice the conversation with a partner. Switch roles and practice it again.

C 🔁 Make a new conversation using other sports.

D 🔁 **GOAL CHECK** ✓ **Describe activities happening now**

Talk to a partner. What are your family and friends doing now?

Listening

A 🔊 **21** Listen to the phone calls. The people are talking about _____ .

a. what they usually do

b. what they are doing at the moment

c. both

▲ go to the movies

▲ go ice skating

▲ study

▲ go to a ball game

▲ play basketball

▲ fix the roof

B 🔊 **21** Listen again. What do these people usually do? When?

1. Alan and Karen usually _____ on _____ .

2. Khaled usually _____ in the _____ .

3. Liam usually _____ on _____ .

C 🔊 **21** Listen again. What are they doing today?

1. Alan and Karen _____ .

2. Khaled_____ .

3. Liam_____ .

▲ A group of boys play volleyball at sunset.

Pronunciation: Reduced form of *What are you . . .*

A 🔊 **22** Listen to the full form and the reduced form.

B 🔊 **23** Listen and check (✓) the correct column.

	Full form	Reduced form
1. What are you reading?		
2. What are you thinking?		
3. What are you playing?		
4. What are you cooking?		
5. What are you writing?		

C 🔊 **23** Listen again. Repeat the sentences.

D 🔄 Practice this conversation using the reduced form. Repeat the conversation using *eat, read,* and *write*. Replace the underlined words.

A: What are you doing?   **A:** What are you <u>cooking</u>?

B: I'm <u>cooking</u>.   **B:** I'm <u>cooking rice</u>.

Communication

A 🔗 One member of the group mimes a sport. The other members of the group try to guess the sport.

B 🔄 **GOAL CHECK** ✔ **Compare everyday and present-time activities**

Work with a partner. What are you doing now? What do you do at this time on a Sunday?

Are you playing volleyball?

Yes, I am.

Language Expansion: Team sports and individual sports

A Write the following sports in the correct box according to the categories.

> baseball   gymnastics   football   volleyball
> ice hockey   diving   skateboarding   golf

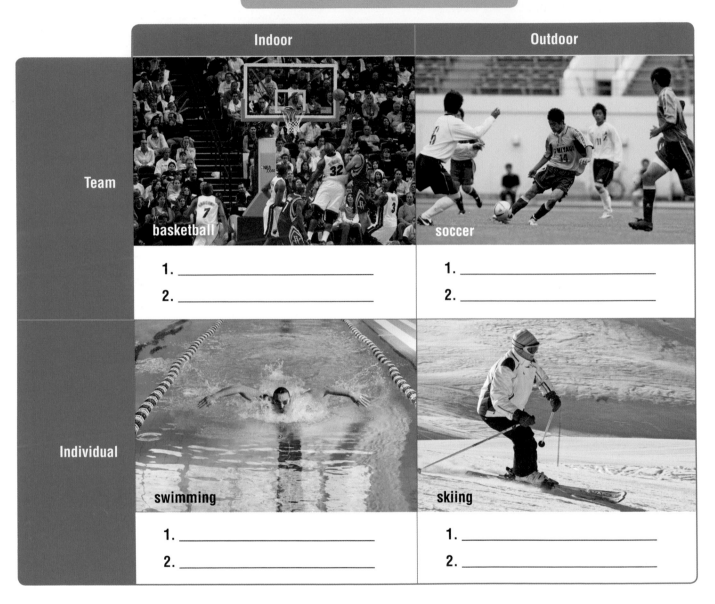

	Indoor	**Outdoor**
Team	basketball 1. _____ 2. _____	soccer 1. _____ 2. _____
Individual	swimming 1. _____ 2. _____	skiing 1. _____ 2. _____

Word Focus

We use *play* for team games—for example, I **play** *soccer*.

We use *go* for individual sports—for example, I **go** *swimming*.

B 👥 Work in groups. Make a chart with new ways to categorize sports. Have the other groups guess the names of your categories.

C Write the names of more sports.

play	soccer,
go	swimming,

Grammar: Stative verbs

Stative verbs			
like	Why do you **like** outdoor sports? I **like** to be outdoors.	know	You **know** I can't swim.
hate	I **hate** indoor sports.	want	I don't **want** to go bungee jumping.
think	I **think** indoor sports are boring.	need	You **need** a lot of equipment.
prefer	Do you **prefer** outdoor sports?	cost	The equipment **costs** a lot of money.

*We usually do not use stative verbs in the present continuous tense.

A Circle the correct form of the verb in parentheses.

1. Skiing is expensive. It (is costing | costs) a lot of money.

2. I (am needing | need) a new soccer shirt.

3. The kids (are playing | play) in the garden at the moment.

4. I don't like team games. I (am preferring | prefer) individual sports.

B Write the correct form of the verb in parentheses.

1. Ashira _____ (not like) to go swimming.

2. I _____ (play) golf right now. Can I call you back?

3. I like rock climbing but my friend _____ (hate) it.

4. Frederick can't come. He _____ (fix) the car.

Conversation

A 🔊 24 Listen to the conversation. Does Adrian want to try rock climbing?

Adrian: Why do you like rock climbing?
Kris: I hate to be indoors all the time.
Adrian: Me too, but it looks dangerous. I don't want to die.
Kris: Me neither! That's why we use ropes.
Adrian: Do you need a lot of equipment?
Kris: Yes, you do, and it costs a lot of money.
Adrian: So it's expensive and dangerous! Well, I think it's a crazy sport. Definitely not for me.

B 🗣 Practice the conversation with a partner. Switch roles and practice it again. Then change the sport and make a new conversation.

C 🗣 **GOAL CHECK** ✓ **Talk about favorite sports**

Tell a partner about your favorite sport. Say why you like it.

> **Real Language**
>
> We say *me too* to agree with a positive statement and *me neither* to agree with a negative statement.

Reading

A Lewis Pugh is an activist who does remarkable things to call attention to **environmental** problems. Look at the photos. Match what he and his team are doing to the photos.

1. _____ 2. _____

3. _____ 4. _____

a. He is swimming.   c. They are hiking.
b. He is speaking.   d. They are rowing.

B 🗘 Read the article with a partner. Underline the sentences with stative verbs.

C Circle **T** for *true* or **F** for *false*.

1. Lewis Pugh is not a very good swimmer.   T F

2. Mt. Everest is the tallest mountain on Earth.   T F

3. Lake Imja is at the bottom of Mt. Everest.   T F

4. A glacier is really the same thing as a lake.   T F

5. Lewis Pugh thinks that people can protect the environment.   T F

WORD BANK

environment where we live; what is around us; the air, land, sea
glacier a huge area of moving ice
global warming a rise in the earth's temperature causing the climate to change
melting becoming water because of heat

TED Ideas worth spreading

Lewis Pugh Adventurer/Environmentalist

MY MIND-SHIFTING EVEREST SWIM

The following article is about Lewis Pugh. After Unit 6, you'll have the opportunity to watch some of Pugh's TED Talk and learn more about his idea worth spreading.

Lewis Pugh is a famous swimmer, but not in the way you might think. In 2007 he swam across the North Pole in water that was so cold his fingers were frozen. Why did Pugh do this? Well, he wants people to pay attention to **global warming** and the problems it is causing.

As a boy, Lewis visited national parks and he learned how fragile and amazing the Earth is. Now he wants to protect the Earth and draw attention to the problems facing it. He decided to swim in water near the North Pole to bring attention to the **melting glaciers** and icecap. Lewis said that the swim was so scary and painful that it would be his last time swimming in freezing water. But when he heard about Lake Imja, near Mt. Everest, high in the Himalayas, he decided to swim in cold water again.

Mt. Everest is the tallest mountain in the world and swimming there is very difficult. It's so high that it's hard to breathe. You feel sick and your head hurts. Because of global warming, glaciers on Mt. Everest are melting and leaving lakes behind, like Lake Imja. This means there's less water for people who need it in nearby countries like China, India, Pakistan, and Bangladesh.

Lewis says he learned two lessons from swimming at Mt. Everest. First, he learned that people can unintentionally do a lot of damage. We do things that hurt the Earth because we know no other way to live. Second, he learned that if we change the way we think, we can do things we didn't think were possible. We can all do something to protect our environment if we change the way we think and think more about our future.

"I heard about the Himalayas and the melting of the glaciers because of climate change."

"Very few things are impossible to achieve if we really put our whole minds to it."

– Lewis Pugh

A lake created by a melted glacier in the Himalayas

Communication

A Match the equipment to the activity. Write the correct number.

1. a ball _____ playing soccer

2. boots _____ ice hockey

3. a bathing suit _____ hiking

4. a backpack _____ swimming

5. skates _____ mountain climbing

B Complete the sentences with the correct verbs. Use the words in the box.

fishing climbing
swimming jogging

1. We love the water. We are going _____ tomorrow.

2. Ahmed wants to catch and eat some shrimp. He is going _____.

3. They like the mountains. They are going _____ this weekend.

4. Jill would like to exercise in the park. She is going _____ today.

C Lewis Pugh swims in dangerous conditions. What other sports can be dangerous? How are they dangerous? Have you ever played a dangerous sport? Which one? Discuss with a partner.

"We all got down onto the ice, and I then got into my swimming costume and I dived into the sea. I have never in my life felt anything like that moment. I could barely breathe. I was gasping for air."

Writing

A Read Lewis Pugh's quote. Then write an e-mail to a friend about a dangerous sport that you'd like to try.

B **GOAL CHECK** ✔ **Discuss adventures**

Share your e-mail with a partner. How are they the same? How are they different?

cheese rolling

Before You Watch

A 🔄 Which of these unusual sports would you like to try? Why? Discuss with a partner.

While You Watch

A ▶️ Fill in the blanks. Use the words in the box. Watch the video and check your answers.

> injuries   cold
> spectators   winner

▲ octopush

1. The first _____ of the day is Craig Brown.

2. One year, one of the cheeses went into the _____.

3. It's not just spectators who get injured—competitors do as well, especially when it's _____ or there hasn't been much rain.

4. Cheese-rolling spectator: "It's when the ground is really hard . . . that's when the _____ are going to happen."

▲ sepak takraw

After You Watch

A 🔄 Discuss these questions with a partner.

1. Why do you think people join the cheese-rolling race?

2. Do they want the cheese?

3. Do they want to have fun?

4. Are they crazy?

Communication

A 🔄 Role-play the following situation.

Student A is a competitor in the cheese-rolling race.

Student B interviews him or her.

> Why do you come?

> Where do you come from?

Destinations

Angkor in Cambodia was a "lost" city, but
now the ruins are a tourist destination
and World Heritage site.

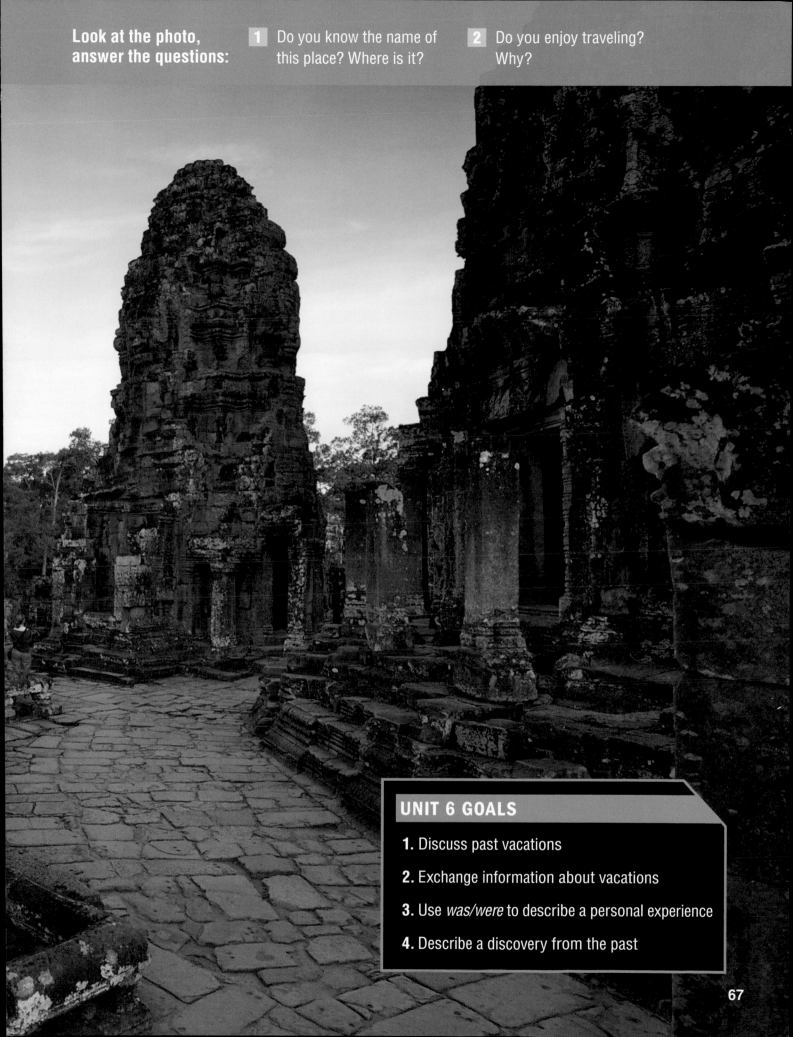

Look at the photo, answer the questions:

1 Do you know the name of this place? Where is it?

2 Do you enjoy traveling? Why?

UNIT 6 GOALS

1. Discuss past vacations

2. Exchange information about vacations

3. Use *was/were* to describe a personal experience

4. Describe a discovery from the past

67

visit places of interest _____

take a bus tour _____

check into the hotel _____

rent a car _____

take photos _____

pack/unpack suitcases _____

buy souvenirs _____

Vocabulary

A Match the photos to an action from the box. Write the numbers.

B Which of these activities do you do *before* and *during* your vacation?

Before	During

C Write other things you do before and during a vacation. Share your ideas with the class.

Grammar: Simple past tense

Simple past tense	
Statement	He **rented** a car on his trip to Europe last November.
Negative	I **didn't have** a reservation yesterday.
Yes/No questions	**Did they go** to Asia last year?
Short answers	Yes, they **did.**/No, they **didn't.**
Information questions	Where **did** you **go** for your vacation last year?

*We use the simple past tense to talk about completed actions or conditions.

*Some verbs are regular in the simple past tense. They have an *-ed* ending.		*Some verbs are irregular in the simple past tense. They have many different forms.	
learn — learned	travel — traveled	eat — ate	tell — told
arrive — arrived	want — wanted	buy — bought	leave — left
play — played	need — needed	fly — flew	say — said
ask — asked	help — helped	know — knew	see — saw
		go — went	take — took

A Unscramble the questions and answers. Use your notebook.

1. **Q:** to Europe Did you go year? last
   A: to we No, went America.

2. **Q:** did buy you those Where souvenirs?
   A: them bought in We Boston.

B Fill in the blanks using the simple past tense of the words in parentheses.

Normally we go to Spain for our vacation, but this year we
(1) _____ (not go). Instead, we (2) _____ (decide)
to go somewhere different, and we (3) _____ (choose)
Dubai in the United Arab Emirates. We (4) _____ (stay) at
the Burj Al Arab hotel – "The Best Hotel in the Middle East." There are
nine restaurants in the hotel, but we (5) _____ (not eat) in
all the restaurants. And of course, the shopping was fantastic. We
(6) _____ (buy) lots of clothes and a few souvenirs. We
also (7) _____ (rent) a car and (8) _____ (go)
to the desert. It is really beautiful, and we (9) _____ (take)
hundreds of photos. It was an excellent vacation.

▲ The Burj Al Arab hotel in Dubai

Conversation

A 🔊 25 Listen to the conversation. How long did Maria stay in Venice?

Christine: Hey, I love that <u>scarf</u>, Maria. Where did you buy it?
Maria: I bought it in <u>Italy</u>. We went to <u>Italy</u> for our vacation last year.
Christine: Wow! Sounds cool. Did you go to <u>Rome</u>?
Maria: No, we flew directly to <u>Venice</u>. I wanted to see the <u>Doge's Palace</u>.
Christine: How long did you stay there?
Maria: We stayed for <u>five</u> nights.
Christine: Lucky you!

B 🔁 Practice the conversation with a partner. Switch roles and practice it again.

C 🔁 Practice the conversation again and change the underlined words. You can use the information in the chart to help you, or use your own ideas.

Country	Italy	United States	Great Britain
Capital	Rome	Washington, D.C.	London
Other city	Venice	Orlando	Edinburgh
Place of special interest	Doge's Palace	Disney World	The Castle

D 🔁 **GOAL CHECK** ✔ **Discuss past vacations**

Take turns with a partner talking about a vacation you took.

Listening

A 🔊 **26** Listen to the conversation. Circle the correct answer.

1. Chen is telling his friend about _____ .

   a. his vacation   **b.** his hobby   **c.** his work

2. His friend is _____ .

   a. bored   **b.** interested   **c.** tired

B 🔊 **26** Listen again. Circle **T** for *true* or **F** for *false*. Correct the false statements in your notebook.

1. Chen went to Oklahoma.   **T**   **F**
2. He visited five theme parks.   **T**   **F**
3. He didn't like Sea World.   **T**   **F**
4. He went to the Spider-Man™ ride.   **T**   **F**
5. He visited Islands of Adventure.   **T**   **F**
6. He didn't try the Incredible Hulk Coaster.   **T**   **F**

Pronunciation: Sounds of *-ed* endings

A 🔊 **27** Listen. Check (✓) the correct boxes in the chart to the left. Then listen again and repeat.

	/t/	/d/	/ɪd/
packed	✓		
traveled		✓	
wanted			✓
arrived			
played			
needed			
asked			
helped			
visited			
rented			
liked			

B 🔊 **28** Listen to the sentences and check (✓) the pronunciation of the *-ed* ending.

	/d/	/t/	/ɪd/
We **checked** into the hotel.			
I **packed** my bags.			
He **traveled** to Europe.			
They **stayed** at an expensive hotel.			

C 🔊 **28** Listen again and repeat the sentences.

Communication

A 🔊 Read the travel blogs on the next page. Fill in the gaps with the past tense of the verbs in parentheses.

From Zanzibar to Zebras

Africa » Tanzania » Dar es Salaam » Zamzibar » Arusha

Read full story | Subscribe

December 12th, 2014

Day 1 __Arrived__ (arrive) in Dar es Salaam. _____ (check) into hotel. _____ (unpack) suitcases. Went swimming.

Day 2 _____ (take) boat to the island of Zanzibar.

Days 3–5 _____ (sunbathe) on the beach. _____ (go) diving.

Day 6 _____ (fly) to Arusha. Saw Kilimanjaro. It's BIG!

Days 7–10 _____ (take) a safari tour. _____ (see) hundreds of wild animals. Took lots of photos.

Day 11 _____ (return) to Arusha. _____ (buy) souvenirs. Took plane to Dar es Salaam and then flew home. Great trip.

Mexico: Beaches and Pyramids

Mexico » Mexico City » Cancun » Tulum » Merida

Read full story | Subscribe

December 18th, 2014

Day 1 __Arrived__ (arrive) in Mexico City. _____ (take) subway to Chapultepec Park. _____ (go) to zoo.

Day 2 _____ (rent) a car. _____ (visit) the Pyramid of the Sun.

Days 3–5 _____ (fly) to Cancun. _____ (go) to the beach.

Day 6 Visited ruins at Tulum. _____ (watch) traditional dance show.

Day 7 Colonial city of Merida. Took a bus tour of the city. _____ (drink) hot chocolate in market.

Day 8 _____ (return) to Mexico City. Flew home.

B 🔗 Choose one blog. Take turns with a partner asking each other questions about your vacation.

> **Where did you go next?**

> **What did you do?**

> **How long did you stay there?**

> **Did you enjoy it? Why?**

C ♻ **GOAL CHECK** ✓ **Exchange information about vacations**

Join another pair of students. Tell them about your partner's vacation from the activity above.

---

fly – flew   sunbathe – sunbathed
watch – watched   drink – drank

Adjectives	Emphatic adjectives
good/nice	excellent outstanding magnificent amazing
bad	awful terrible horrible
interesting	fascinating
tiring	exhausting
dirty	filthy
clean	spotless
big	enormous huge

Language Expansion: Emphatic adjectives

A Write two or three emphatic adjectives below each picture.

_____ _____

_____ _____

B Use emphatic adjectives to complete the text.

We had an (1) _____ vacation. We visited six European countries in six days. My favorite country was Italy. Rome is a (2) _____ city. There is so much to see: museums, churches, ruins. We stayed in a (3) _____ hotel. Everything about it was perfect. It had an (4) _____ swimming pool and very friendly people.

Grammar: Simple past tense of *to be*

Simple past tense of *to be*	
Statement	I **was** exhausted.
Negative	The food **wasn't** great.
Information questions	Why **was** your vacation awful?
Yes/No questions	**Were** they tired?
Short answers	No, they **weren't.**

A Match the questions and the answers.

1. Were you tired? _____
2. Where were they? _____
3. Was the weather good? _____
4. Was he late? _____
5. Were the rooms clean? _____

a. No, he wasn't. He was on time.
b. They were in Peru.
c. No, they weren't. They were filthy.
d. Yes, I was. I was exhausted.
e. Yes, it was. It was excellent.

B Complete the sentences with *was* or *were*.

1. We didn't enjoy our vacation. The weather _____ very bad.

2. How _____ the food?

3. _____ you tired when you got home?

4. I _____ really interested in the ruins. They were amazing.

5. _____ the hotel clean?

C Complete the sentences with the correct forms of *to be*.

Last year we went diving at Pulau Sipadan, Malaysia.

It (1) _____ amazing! There (2) _____

lots of turtles, and we saw some hammerhead sharks,

as well. We also went to Barracuda Point, but unfortunately,

there (3) _____ any barracuda. It (4) _____

the wrong time of year. We stayed at the Dive Center and

the food (5) _____ excellent. The rooms

(6) _____ spotless.

▲ A diver in Pulau Sipadan

D ⟳ Write three questions about exercise **C** to ask your partner.

Conversation

A ◀)) 29 Listen to the conversation. What was good about the vacation?

Alex: How was your vacation?

Mike: It was terrible.

Alex: Why? What happened?

Mike: Well, first of all, the weather was <u>bad</u>. It rained nonstop for two weeks.

Alex: Oh, no.

Mike: And the hotel was <u>dirty</u>. It was full of cockroaches.

Alex: Yuck! And how was the food?

Mike: Actually, the food was <u>good</u>.

Alex: Well, at least you enjoyed something.

Mike: Not really. I had a bad stomach and couldn't eat. Some vacation!

B ⟳ Practice the conversation with a partner. Switch roles and practice it again.

C ⟳ Practice again and change the underlined adjectives to emphatic adjectives.

The weather was awful.

The food was excellent.

D ⟳ **GOAL CHECK** ✔ **Use *was/were* to describe a personal experience**

Tell a partner about a good or bad experience you had.

Reading

A Look at the black and white photos. When do you think these photos were taken?

B Read the article. Underline the emphatic adjectives.

C Underline the regular simple past verbs and circle the irregulars.

D Answer the questions.

1. Did Hiram Bingham discover Inca ruins in Ollantaytambo? _____
   _____

2. How much did he pay Arteaga? _____
   _____

3. Was the climb to Machu Picchu easy?
   _____

4. Where did they eat? _____
   _____

▲ A man stands at the walls of the main temple.

Word Focus

hut = a small house
ruins = old buildings that have
fallen down
to clear = to cut down

Machu Picchu, Peru

THE CRADLE OF THE
INCA EMPIRE

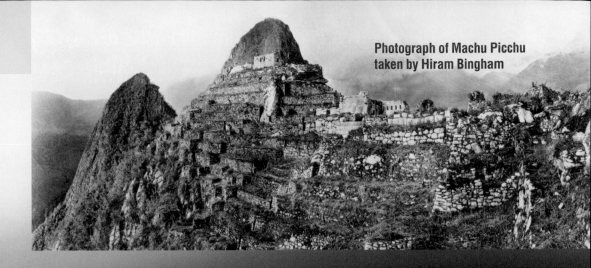

Most people travel for vacations, but some people travel to explore and discover new places. In 1911, Hiram Bingham, an American archaeologist, traveled to Peru where he discovered Machu Picchu, the lost city of the Incas. Read his report of the discovery.

In 1911, I went to Cuzco in Peru looking for ancient Inca **ruins.** We left Cuzco and traveled to the modern city of Urubamba. We then continued down the Urubamba River until we came to the beautiful little town of Ollantaytambo. We continued down the river, and six days after we left Cuzco, we arrived at a place called Mandorpampa. A man came and introduced himself as Arteaga, and I asked him about ruins. He told us of some ruins in the mountains, called Machu Picchu. I offered to pay him 50 cents per day to take us to the ruins, and he agreed.

The next day, we crossed the river and began an exhausting climb. At noon we arrived at a little grass **hut.** The people there were very friendly and gave us some boiled potatoes and cool water. The view was magnificent, the water was delicious, but there were no ruins. However, we continued upward until at last we arrived on top of the mountain. Immediately, we found some ancient Inca walls made of white stone. I knew at once that this was a truly amazing discovery.

I returned to Machu Picchu in 1912, and we began **to clear** the forest. We started to see the ruins, and they were outstanding. The walls are made from enormous stones, and as we continued to clear the forest, we discovered more and more ruins. At last, the lost city of Machu Picchu appeared before us.

The Pyramids of Giza

Communication

A Work with a group and fill in as much information in the chart as you can.

	Stonehenge	Pyramids of Giza	A ruin in your country
Where is it?	in England		
What was it?	a burial ground		
Who built it?	Ancient Britons		
When was it built?	3000 BCE–2000 BCE		

B Share your information with the class and write in any new information from classmates.

Writing

A Write a travel blog about one of the places from the chart. Use your notebook for extra space if needed.

_____

_____

_____

_____

B **GOAL CHECK** ✓ **Describe a discovery from the past**

Talk to a partner about a discovery from the past that you know about.

Before You Watch

A Fill in the blanks. Use the words in the box to complete the video summary.

| tourists | environment |
| quiet | business |

Video summary

When Hiram Bingham discovered Machu Picchu, it was a (1) _____

place. Now, many (2) _____ go to Machu Picchu every day. Some

people say it is good for (3) _____, but other people say it is bad for

the (4) _____ .

While You Watch

A ▶ Watch the video. Circle **T** for *true* and **F** for *false*.

1. Machu Picchu is a popular tourist destination. **T** **F**

2. Machu Picchu is sometimes known as the Lost Town of the Incas. **T** **F**

3. Conservationists think tourism is good for Machu Picchu. **T** **F**

4. Jose wants more people to come to Machu Picchu. **T** **F**

After You Watch

A 🗘 Discuss these questions with a partner.

1. What are the big tourist attractions in your country?

2. Are there any problems with tourism in your country? What are they?

3. Do you think tourism is good or bad? Give reasons.

> **Tourists buy souvenirs and stay in hotels.**

> **That's good. It brings money to the country.**

TEDTALKS

Before You Watch

A 🔁 Look at the pictures. Which of these places would you like to visit? Why? Research the places if needed. Tell a partner. Do you share the same answers?

Greenland

Patagonia, Chile

Mt. Everest, Nepal

Santa Cruz, Argentina

B Use the words in the box to complete the TED Talk summary.

symbolic	humility	aggressive
Sherpas	debrief	sustainable

WORD BANK
aggressive to do something with a lot of force
battleground a place where there are a lot of problems or conflict
debrief to talk about something after it is done
humility thinking you are not more important than other people or things
instability a situation that can change at any time
Sherpas people who live in the Himalayas and work as mountain guides
sustainable something that will last a long time
symbolic representing something
tactical something that is smartly planned

Lewis Pugh's idea worth spreading is that we can do something to stop climate change; we just need to take it seriously. That's why he swam across Lake Imja, a place that should be made of ice. Watch Pugh's full TED Talk at TED.com.

TED Talk Summary

Lewis Pugh swims in cold places because it is _____ of saving the environment. He wants Earth to be _____ , or around forever. Lewis decided to swim in a lake high on Mt. Everest in the Himalayas. _____ helped him climb the big mountain to Lake Imja. After a failed first attempt, Lewis had a _____ to discuss the best way to swim at 5,300 meters (17,400 feet) above sea level. He is usually very _____ when he swims because he wants to finish quickly and get out of the cold water. But this time he showed _____ and swam slowly.

C 👥 Look closely at the pictures in exercise **A** again. All of these places used to be completely covered in snow and ice. Discuss the following questions as a group.

What do you think is happening to the snow and ice in the pictures? Why? What do you think you will see in the TED Talk?

While You Watch

A ▶ Watch the TED Talk. Put the quotes in order. Write the number in the boxes provided.

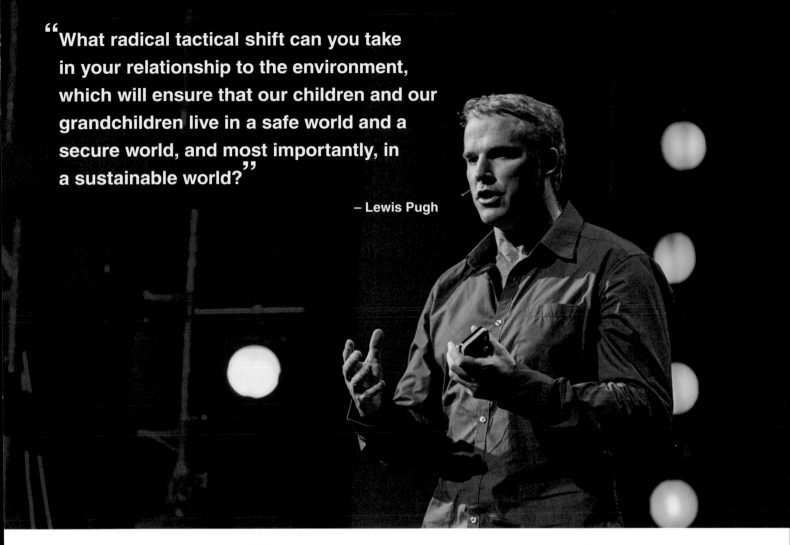

> "What radical tactical shift can you take in your relationship to the environment, which will ensure that our children and our grandchildren live in a safe world and a secure world, and most importantly, in a sustainable world?"
>
> – Lewis Pugh

☐ "And I remember getting out of the water and my hands feeling so painful and looking down at my fingers, and my fingers were literally the size of sausages."

☐ "I heard about this lake, Lake Imja. This lake has been formed in the last couple of years because of the melting of the glacier."

☐ "And so I decided to walk up to Mt. Everest, the highest mountain on this earth, and go and do a symbolic swim underneath the summit of Mt. Everest."

☐ "And I swam across the lake. And I can't begin to tell you how good I felt when I came to the other side."

After You Watch

A Watch the TED Talk again. Circle the correct answer for each question.

1. What are the Himalayas?	big lakes	big mountains
2. How long did Lewis swim at the North Pole?	19 minutes	30 minutes
3. What is melting in the Himalayas?	glaciers	lakes
4. How many people depend on water from the Himalayas?	2 billion	1 million
5. What is the world's population?	9 billion	6.8 billion

B Fill in the names of the places from the words in the box.

Lake Imja	North Pole	Bangladesh
Mt. Everest	Himalayas	

1. In 2007, Lewis Pugh swam at the _____.

2. The glaciers in the _____ are melting.

3. The highest mountain on Earth is _____.

4. _____ is very high, near the top of Mt. Everest.

5. China, India, Pakistan, and _____ are countries near the Himalayas.

C Use the emphatic adjectives to complete the sentences.

exhausting	fascinating	enormous
excellent	awful	

1. Mt. Everest isn't small. It's a(n) _____ mountain.

2. His story wasn't boring. It was _____.

3. Lewis Pugh survived his North Pole swim. He must be a(n)

_____ swimmer.

4. Swimming for a very long time, especially in cold conditions, isn't easy.

It is _____.

5. When Lewis Pugh first tried the swim, he had to stop. He felt

_____.

A melting ice field

D Lewis Pugh completed his amazing swims to call attention to the problem of global warming. Here are some things caused by global warming. Write the correct captions under the pictures. Have you seen any of these things before? Give examples and discuss with a partner.

Effects of Global Warming

Animals in Danger	Huge Storms
No Water	Floods

1. _____

2. _____

3. _____

4. _____

E Make a list of things of things you can do to protect the environment. Discuss as a group. Share your list with other groups.

Challenge! Look at the pictures from exercise **D** again. Research other effects of global warming. Make a list. Then research what your country is doing to address the problem of global warming. Is it enough? Write an essay with your ideas to share with the class.

Communication

Wolves may howl to let other wolf packs know to stay away from their territory, or just to let others know where they are.

UNIT 7 GOALS

1. Talk about personal communication

2. Exchange contact information

3. Describe characteristics and qualities

4. Compare different types of communication

1. _____

Vocabulary

A Label the pictures. Use the words in the box.

> e-mail   fax   smartphone   TV   letter
> newspaper ad   social media   text message

B Write the words from exercise **A** in the correct column.

	Inexpensive	Expensive
fast		smartphone
slow	letter	

Grammar: Verbs with direct and indirect objects

(Subject) + verb	Indirect object	Direct object
I sent	Mike	an e-mail.
My parents bought	me	a smartphone.
I am writing	Helen	a text message.
Find	me	his number, please.
I didn't fax	him	the report.
Give	me	a call.

2. _____

3. _____

4. _____

5. _____

6. _____

7. _____

8. _____

A Unscramble the words to write sentences. Underline the indirect objects.

1. sent   a   I   fax.   Barbara

   _____

2. sent   My   brother   an   me   e-mail.

   _____

3. address.   me   his   Find   e-mail

   _____

4. new   Jim   a   computer.   I   bought

   _____

5. a   your   mom   Give   call.

   _____

Irregular past tense	
Present	**Past**
buy	bought
send	sent
write	wrote
find	found
get	got

B Read the situations and make requests. Use the verbs in parentheses.

Situation	Request
1. You lost your friend's phone number.	(send) *Please send me your phone number.*
2. You want your friend to call his father.	(give) _____
3. You want your parents to buy your sister a printer.	(buy) _____
4. You want your friend to pay you by check.	(write) _____

C 🔁 Ask your partner how, and how often, they communicate with other people.

Conversation

A 🔊 2 Listen to the conversation. How does Ken communicate with Chris?

Ken: Hey, Chris. I sent you <u>an e-mail</u> yesterday and you didn't answer.
Chris: <u>E-mail</u>? What <u>e-mail</u>? You didn't send me an <u>e-mail</u>.
Ken: Come on! You got it. Then I sent you <u>a text message</u>.
Chris: <u>Text message</u>? What <u>text message</u>? You didn't send me a <u>text message</u>, either. Honest!
Ken: OK, well you've got no excuses now. Where's the $15 you owe me?
Chris: $15? What $15?

> **Real Language**
>
> We can use *Come on!* to show impatience.

B 🔁 Practice the conversation with a partner. Switch roles and practice it again.

C 🔁 Change the underlined words and practice it again.

D 🔁 **GOAL CHECK** ✔ **Talk about personal communication**

Write a list of types of personal communication that you use and another list of types of personal communication that you don't use. Compare your lists with a partner.

Listening

A 🔊 **3** Listen to the radio program. Circle the correct answer.

This is a _____ .

a. talk show   **b.** music show   **c.** call-in program

B 🔊 **3** Listen again and complete the chart.

Phone number	
Fax number	
E-mail address	
Text message (SMS) address	
Mailing address	

Written	Pronounced
@	at
-	hyphen
<u>Sydney</u>	underscore
/	slash
\	backslash
St.	street
Ave.	avenue

C 🔁 Below is the contact information of some famous places. Take turns reading them aloud with a partner using the correct pronunciation.

1. Bennelong Point, Sydney, New South Wales, Australia. Tel. + 61 29250 7111 www.sydneyoperahouse.com e-mail: infodesk@sydneyoperahouse.com

2. 1600 Pennsylvania Ave. NW, Washington DC, 20500, USA. Tel. 1 202 456 1111 www.whitehouse.gov e-mail: comments@whitehouse.gov

3. 5 Avenue Anatole France, 75007, Paris, France. Tel. 33 08 92 70 12 39 www.tour-eiffel.fr

Pronunciation: /b/ and /v/, /l/ and /r/

A 🔊 **4** Listen and circle the word that you hear.

/b/	/v/		/l/	/r/
1. bat	vat	**1.** alive	arrive
2. berry	very	**2.** blush	brush
3. best	vest	**3.** flee	free
4. ban	van	**4.** fly	fry
5. boat	vote	**5.** lane	rain
6. bowels	vowels	**6.** lead	read
7. bale	veil	**7.** lice	rice
8. bent	vent	**8.** light	right
9. best	vest	**9.** long	wrong
10. bet	vet	**10.** play	pray

Real Language

When we want someone to repeat something, we can say: *Sorry, I missed that* or *Could you repeat that, please?*

When we want someone to say a word letter by letter, we can say: *Could you spell that, please?*

B 🔁 Take turns reading one of the words from each pair to your partner. Your partner has to identify which word you read.

Communication

A Write your contact information in column one of the chart.

B 👥 Ask three of your classmates for their contact information. Complete the chart.

	Me	Classmate 1	Classmate 2	Classmate 3
Name				
Home phone number				
Cell phone number				
E-mail address				
Mailing address				

C 🔁 **GOAL CHECK** ✓ **Exchange contact information**

Give the contact details of a friend or family member to a partner.

▲ sight

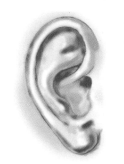

▲ hearing

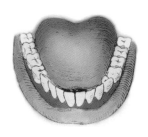

▲ taste

▲ smell

▲ touch

Language Expansion: The senses

With the senses, we perceive (*see, notice, feel*) characteristics and qualities of people, animals, places, and things.

A 🔁 Look at the senses to the left. Discuss the following question with a partner. What senses do you use to identify these characteristics?

▲ sweet   ▲ loud   ▲ soft   ▲ green

▲ dirty   ▲ bad   ▲ salty   ▲ wet

B 🔁 Work with a partner to make a list of other things you can perceive with your senses.

Grammar: Sensory verbs

Subject	Verb	Adjective
The food	**smells**	delicious.
It	**feels**	soft.
You	**look**	cold.
It	**tastes**	salty.
He	**sounds**	tired.

*Sensory verbs are stative verbs.
*They are usually followed by an adjective.
*They are not used in the simple progressive tense.

▲ People in this market in Phonsavan, Laos, use many senses at the same time.

A Complete the sentences with sensory verbs.

1. That car can't be safe. It _____ very old.

2. Listen to the CD player! It _____ terrible.

3. What are you cooking? It _____ delicious.

4. Hey, you changed your hair. It _____ great.

5. I don't like these French fries. They _____ too salty.

6. I prefer this sweater. It _____ soft.

B Take turns with a partner. Describe the photo above by making statements with *looks*, *sounds*, *tastes*, *smells*, *feels*, and an adjective.

Conversation

A 🔊 5 Listen to the conversation. What's wrong with Bill and Susan's milk?

Susan: I think there is something wrong with this <u>milk</u>.
Bill: It looks OK to me.
Susan: Smell it! It smells <u>terrible</u>.
Bill: Mmm. It doesn't smell too bad. How does it taste?
Susan: I'm not going to taste it!
Bill: OK, let me try. Ugh, you're right. It tastes <u>awful</u>.

B Practice the conversation with a partner. Switch roles and practice it again.

C Change the underlined words and make a new conversation.

D **GOAL CHECK** ✔ **Describe characteristics and qualities**

Work with a partner. Use sensory verbs to describe your classroom and your classmates.

Reading

A Animals use all their senses, but for many animals, one of the senses is the most important. Check (✓) one box for each animal and compare with a partner.

	By sight	By sound	By smell
1. dogs			✓
2. ants			
3. whales			
4. peacocks			
5. wolves			
6. bees			

B Read the article. With a partner, discuss these questions: Are dolphins intelligent? Do they have feelings? Do the same for the other animals listed in exercise **A**.

C Read the sentences. Are they true or false? Circle **T** for *true* or **F** for *false*.

1. People are self-aware.   T F

2. Scientists do experiments to gain information.   T F

3. When two people talk, it is **interspecies** communication. T F

4. When you use your brain, you are using cognition. T F

5. You usually recognize people you have never seen before. T F

6. Some animals whistle to communicate.   T F

WORD BANK

ability what someone or something is able to do
cognition mental activities (thinking, understanding, learning, remembering)
experiment scientific test
interspecies between species
recognize to know because of previous experience
self-aware aware of oneself
whistle high, loud sound

TED Ideas worth spreading

Diana Reiss Scientist

THE INTERSPECIES INTERNET? AN IDEA IN PROGRESS

The following article is about Diana Reiss. After Unit 9, you'll have the opportunity to watch some of Reiss and her colleagues' TED Talk and learn more about their idea worth spreading.

What happens when you give a dolphin a mirror or a computer keyboard? Just ask Diana Reiss. She studies the **cognition** and communication of dolphins. Scientists believe that dolphins and other animals are **self-aware** and have emotions. They are able to think, learn, and remember.

Diana Reiss showed these **abilities** in her research with dolphins and elephants. Reiss used a mirror in her studies. The animals **recognized** themselves in the mirror. That shows that they are self-aware.

Reiss also made a special keyboard that could work underwater. The keyboard had keys that the dolphins could touch. When touched, the computer would make a whistle and the dolphins got a fun object or activity. In the **experiment,** the dolphins learned to use the keyboard all by themselves. They played with the keyboard, copied the **whistles,** and learned which keys to touch to get what they wanted.

Diana Reiss's keyboard experiment showed that dolphins have cognitive abilities and can use them to communicate. But that experiment was many years ago. Now, she is interested in what today's technology can show us about animal minds. What do you think of an orangutan using an iPad? Or other animals being connected through the Internet?

Many scientists think dolphins have emotions and recognize themselves.

"How do we explore intelligence in this animal that's so different from us?"

– Diana Reiss

Dolphins can communicate with each other using a keyboard. Do you think they can communicate with people?

Writing

A 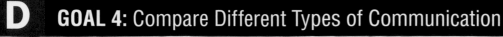 What type of communication would you use in these situations? Text message, e-mail, letter, or social media? Fill in the first column and then ask your partner. Discuss any differences.

You want to . . .	Me	My partner
1. . . . send a photo to your parents.		
2. . . . thank your grandmother for a birthday present.		
3. . . . keep in touch with some friends in Brazil.		
4. . . . invite a friend to do something with you.		
5. . . . send an assignment to your teacher.		

Hi. HRU?

GREAT. WRUD?

NOTHING. WANNA GO TO THE MOVIES TN?

IDUNNO. GOTTA FINISH MY PROJECT.

OK LMK.

OK CU LATER.

B People often use abbreviations. Do you understand these messages? Which situation from exercise **A** do they match? With a partner, write a new text conversation. Explain your abbreviations to the class.

Communication

A With a partner, make a list of some of the other ways humans communicate. Then pick an animal and list the way it communicates.

B | GOAL CHECK ✔ Compare different types of communication

With your partner, compare human communication with animal communication. How are they the same? How are they different? Share your ideas with the class.

An elephant and rhinoceros
in the African bush

Before You Watch

A Match the words to the definitions.

1. conservationist _____
2. increase _____
3. decrease _____
4. to track _____

a. to follow wild animals
b. a person who protects wild animals
c. to get (or make) bigger
d. to get (or make) smaller

While You Watch

A ▶ Watch the video. Circle **T** for *true* and **F** for *false*.

1. In the video, you see lions.   T   F
2. Louis Liebenberg is trying to collect information
   about the animals.   T   F
3. The Bushmen and the conservationists speak the
   same language.   T   F
4. The small computer that the Bushmen use is called
   the Cyber Tracker.   T   F
5. Louis Liebenberg makes maps from the information.   T   F

After You Watch

A 🗘 The Cyber Tracker is a quick way of recording information about wild animals.
Can you think of other uses for the Cyber Tracker? Discuss with a partner.

As global trade has increased, port cities like Singapore have become more and more important.

Look at the photo, answer the questions:

1 Why do you think shipping ports are important?

2 Are you looking forward to the future? Why?

UNIT 8 GOALS

1. Talk about plans

2. Discuss long- and short-term plans

3. Make weather predictions

4. Discuss the future

Vocabulary

A Number the pictures to match the phrases from the box.

1. study for the next test	4. buy a new car	7. buy my own house
2. get a new job	5. have children	8. speak English fluently
3. do the laundry	6. clean the house	

B Write the plans from exercise **A** in the correct column.

Short-term plans	Long-term plans

> I don't want to have children now. I'm too young.

> I need to buy a new car. My car is really old.

C 🔁 Number the long-term plans in order of importance to you (1 for the most important plan). Compare your list with a partner's list. Give reasons.

Grammar: Future—*be going to*

Be going to		
Statements	We**'re going to** buy a new car tomorrow.	
Negatives	He**'s not going to** get a new job next year.	
Yes/No questions	**Are** you **going to** do the laundry this weekend?	Yes, I am. No, I'm not.
Wh- question	When **are** you **going to** pay the phone bill?	On Tuesday.

*We can use *be going to* to talk about our plans for the future.
*We also use these time expressions: *tomorrow, next Saturday / week / year.*

A Match the questions and the answers.

1. Where are you going to have lunch today? _____
2. Are you going to invite Ajay to the party? _____
3. What are you going to do on Saturday? _____
4. When is Nicola going to arrive? _____
5. Is it going to rain this evening? _____

a. Yes, I am. He loves dancing.
b. Maybe. I would take an umbrella.
c. At Luigi's.
d. We're going to go ice skating.
e. Her plane arrives at five o'clock.

B Complete the conversation with *be going to* and the verbs in parentheses.

A: Hey! I just won $100!

B: Wow! What _____ (you do) with it?

A: Well, first, I _____ (buy) my mother some flowers.

B: Great. She _____ (love) those.

A: And then, I _____ (give) my sister $10.

B: And the rest?

A: I _____ (put) it in the bank.

B: _____ (you buy) anything for yourself?

A: Maybe. But not now.

C Look at the pictures on page 96. Take turns asking a partner questions about the phrases.

> When/Where/How/Why are you going to . . . ?

Conversation

A 🔊 **6** Listen to the conversation. Is Kiri going to go to the beach?

Mai: Hi, Kiri. What are you going to do this weekend?

Kiri: Well, I'm going to <u>study for the test</u> and <u>do the laundry</u>. Why? Why do you ask?

Mai: We're going to <u>go to the beach</u>. Do you want to come?

Kiri: Mmm, I'm not sure. I'd love to, but . . . you know . . . work.

Mai: Come on. It's going to be fun!

Kiri: Well, maybe I can <u>study for the test</u> tonight. And I can <u>do the laundry</u> when we come back.

Mai: So you're going to come?

Kiri: Sure!

> Real Language
>
> We can say *Mmm* or *I'm not sure* to show uncertainty.

B Practice the conversation with a partner. Switch roles and practice it again.

C Change the underlined words and practice it again.

D **GOAL CHECK** ✔ **Talk about plans**

Tell a partner your plans for this weekend.

> I'm going to go hiking this weekend.

Listening

A 🔊 7 Listen to the interview with a pop singer. Is he talking about his short-term plans or long-term plans?

B 🔊 7 Listen again and circle **T** for *true* and **F** for *false*.

1. Pedro is going to record his new album in June.	**T**	**F**
2. You can buy Pedro's new album in stores.	**T**	**F**
3. Pedro is going to take a break in the summer.	**T**	**F**
4. Pedro is going to do a world tour this year.	**T**	**F**
5. Alicia is going to have a baby in July.	**T**	**F**
6. The baby isn't going to change Pedro's life.	**T**	**F**
7. Pedro is going to start making a film at the end of the year.	**T**	**F**

C Correct the *false* sentences in exercise **B** in your notebook.

Pronunciation: Reduced form of *going to*

A 🔊 8 Listen and repeat.

B 🔊 9 Listen to the sentence and check (✓) the correct box.

	Full form	**Reduced form**
1. When are you going to finish?	☐	☐
2. They're not going to like it.	☐	☐
3. We're going to leave at three thirty.	☐	☐
4. I'm going to take a shower.	☐	☐
5. Are you going to take a taxi?	☐	☐
6. What are you going to do this weekend?	☐	☐
7. I'm not going to go to the meeting.	☐	☐
8. When is Saleh going to arrive?	☐	☐

C 🔄 Take turns reading the sentences in exercise **B** with either the *full form* or the *reduced form*. Your partner has to say which form you used.

A hang glider soars above Yosemite National Park in the United States.

Communication

A What are your short-term and long-term plans? Check (✓) the correct column.

Short-term plans			
Are you going to . . .	**Yes, I am.**	**I'm not sure.**	**No, I'm not.**
eat out tonight?			
go to a party this weekend?			
play or watch a sport this evening?			
rest this weekend?			

Long-term plans			
Are you going to . . .	**Yes, I am.**	**I'm not sure.**	**No, I'm not.**
start your own business?			
learn another language?			
move to another country?			
buy a new car?			

B 🔁 With a partner, take turns asking and answering the questions in exercise **A.** Then ask a *Wh-* question.

C 🔁 **GOAL CHECK** ✔ **Discuss long- and short-term plans**

Tell a partner your plans for tonight and your plans for the next five years. Use the words in the box to help you.

> Are you going to start your own business?

> Yes, I am.

> What type of business?

> I'm not sure. Maybe a hang gliding school.

> tomorrow   next weekend
> next week   next month
> next year   in five years

▲ raincoat

Language Expansion: Weather conditions

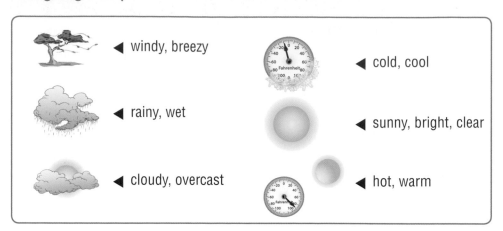

◀ windy, breezy

◀ rainy, wet

◀ cloudy, overcast

◀ cold, cool

◀ sunny, bright, clear

◀ hot, warm

We use adjectives to describe the weather. *Today is **sunny** and **warm**.*

A Complete the sentences. Use the words on this page.

1. It's not going to rain tomorrow. You don't need to take your

   _____ or your _____.

2. Put on your sweater. It's going to be _____ outside.

3. The weather forecast says it's going to be cloudy today. You don't need to

   take your _____.

4. It's going to be _____ and _____ tomorrow,

   so don't forget your sun hat.

▲ umbrella ▲ sunglasses

▲ rain boots ▲ swimsuit

Grammar: *Will* for predictions and immediate decisions

Will		
Statements	I think it **will** rain this afternoon. It **will** be windy tomorrow.	
Negatives	Don't take your sweater. I'm sure it **will not (won't)** be cold.	
Yes/No questions	**Will** it be windy?	Yes, it **will.**/No, it **won't.**

*We use *be going to* and *will* to make predictions.
*We only use *will* to make an immediate decision. **A:** The phone is ringing. **B:** OK, I will answer it.

▲ sun hat ▲ scarf

A Complete the sentences using *will* or *be going to.*

1. **A:** You're looking happy.
   B: Yes, I _____ buy a new car this afternoon.

2. **A:** Oh no! It's starting to rain.
   B: I _____ get an umbrella.

3. **A:** This is heavy.
   B: Wait, I _____ help you.

4. **A:** You have to get up at five o'clock tomorrow.
   B: Yes, I _____ to go to bed early tonight.

▲ sweater

B Rewrite the questions using *be going to* or *will*.

be going to	will
1. Is it going to rain tomorrow?	
2.	Will it be sunny this afternoon?
3. Are we going to have a hot summer this year?	
4.	What will the weather be like on the weekend?
5. Is it going to be overcast tomorrow?	
6.	Will we finish the book before the end of the year?
7. Are temperatures going to rise in the next 100 years?	
8.	Will you get good grades?

C 🔁 With a partner, take turns asking and answering the questions in exercise **B.**

D Write some predictions about your life. Use *be going to* and *will*.

1. I _____ have a happy life.

2. I _____ live to be 100 years old.

3. I _____ find an interesting job.

4. I _____ speak perfect English one day.

Conversation

A 🔊 **10** Listen to the conversation.

Andrew: Do we have everything ready for the beach?
Barbara: Sure. Everything's ready.
Andrew: Do you think it's going to rain?
Barbara: No, they say it's going to be hot.
Andrew: Are you going to take your umbrella?
Barbara: No, I said it's going to be hot. It's not going to rain.
Andrew: No, I mean your beach umbrella for the sun.
Barbara: Oh, I see. Yes, that's a good idea.

B 🔁 Practice the conversation with a partner. Switch roles and practice it again.

C 🔁 Circle the predictions. Change *be going to* to *will* and practice it again.

D 🔁 **GOAL CHECK** ✓ **Make weather predictions**

Talk to a partner. What is the weather like now? What is it going to be like tomorrow?

Reading

A 🔁 Discuss these questions with a partner. Then read and check your answers.

1. What are fossil fuels?

2. What is alternative energy?

B Read the article. Underline *will* and *be going to*.

C Answer the questions.

1. How much energy will we need in 2100?

   _____

2. What are three problems with solar power? _____

   _____

3. What are two problems with wind energy? _____

   _____

4. Does Michael Pacheco think there will be enough energy in the future?

   _____

   _____

D 🔁 How do you think people will get energy in the future? Solar, wind, fossil fuels, or another way? Discuss with a partner.

Word Focus

alternative = something different

cost-effective = something *cost-effective* saves money

renewable = something you can use again and again

ugly = not beautiful

FUTURE ENERGY
WHERE WILL WE GET OUR ENERGY?

We are going to have a big energy problem in the future. Today, the world uses 320 billion kilowatt-hours of energy a day. By 2100, we will use three times as much energy. How will we get the energy? Today, we get a lot of energy from fossil fuels: coal, oil, and natural gas. But fossil fuels are dirty, and they will not last forever. In the long term, we will have to find **alternatives**. We will need **renewable** energy.

SOLAR POWER

Near Leipzig in Germany, there is a field with 33,500 solar panels. It produces enough energy for 1,800 homes. That's a lot of energy! However, there are problems. One problem is that solar energy is expensive, but the price is falling. "Thirty years ago it was **cost-effective** on satellites," says Daniel Shugar, president of PowerLight Corporation. "Today, we can use it for houses and businesses." He says that in the future most houses will have solar panels. There are other problems with solar power. It needs a lot of space, and, of course, it doesn't work at night.

WIND POWER

On a cloudy day in Denmark, a wind turbine is producing clean, renewable electricity. Right now, wind power is the best of the alternative energy sources. But again, there are problems. Some people think wind turbines are **ugly**. And, of course, there are days when there is no wind.

So, how will our grandchildren get their energy? "We're going to need everything we can get from solar, everything we can get from wind," says Michael Pacheco, director of the National Bioenergy Center, part of the National Renewable Energy Laboratory (NREL) in Golden, Colorado. "And still the question is: Can we get enough?"

The surface of Mars

Communication

A Write more questions in the chart. Fill in the first column with your answers, and then ask your partner the questions. Compare and discuss your answers.

In the future, do you think . . .	Me			Partner		
	Yes	Maybe	No	Yes	Maybe	No
1. . . . people will live under the sea?						
2. . . . there will be enough food for everyone?						
3. . . . we will find a cure for cancer?						
4. . . . most houses will have solar panels?						
5. . . . people will travel to Mars?						
6. . . . wars will end?						
7.						
8.						

Writing

A Write when you think these events will happen in your notebook.

In the next 50 years, I think we will find a cure for cancer, maybe most houses will have solar panels, but I don't think people will travel to Mars.

Maybe by 2100 people will . . .

B  **GOAL CHECK** ✓ **Discuss the future**

Join two or three other students and discuss your ideas about the future.

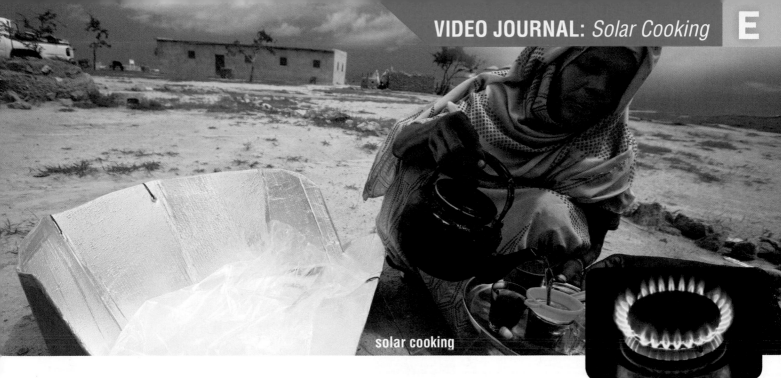
solar cooking

▲ gas

▲ electricity

▲ firewood

▲ solar energy

Before You Watch

A 🔁 Look at the pictures. Discuss these questions with a partner.

1. What fuels can you use to cook food?

2. What fuel do you use to cook food?

While You Watch

A ▶ Watch the video. Check (✓) the correct box.

Benefits of solar ovens	Health	Environmental
1. You don't have to cut down trees.	☐	☐
2. African women don't have to walk a long way to collect firewood.	☐	☐
3. There is no smoke.	☐	☐
4. Solar ovens can be used to make water clean.	☐	☐
5. Solar ovens don't cause pollution.	☐	☐

After You Watch/Communication

A 🔁 With a partner, make a list of what you need to make a solar oven. Write instructions on how to make the oven. Use drawings if needed. Then, role-play the following situation.

Student A
You are running a workshop in Africa. You have to explain the benefits of using solar ovens. Some of the participants have doubts.

Student B
You are a participant in the workshop. Your mother cooked with wood and you cook with wood. You have doubts about changing. Ask questions.

▲ wind

Types of Clothing

In Egypt, Bedouins celebrate a wedding by dancing and wearing festive clothes.

UNIT 9 GOALS

1. Make comparisons

2. Explain preferences

3. Talk about clothing materials

4. Evaluate quality and value

tie   jeans   skirt   shirt
suit   jacket   pants   hat
sneakers   T-shirt   socks
blouse   coat   handbag
shoes   hat   belt   gloves

Vocabulary

A 🔁 Work with a partner and label the pictures with words from the box.

B Underline the adjectives that describe clothes.

1. **a.** Fatima is wearing a heavy, handmade sweater, and she's warm.

   b. Charles is wearing a light, poor-quality coat, and he's cold.

2. **a.** John wore an expensive, formal, business suit to the interview.

   b. Andrew wore a cheap, casual jacket. Guess who got the job!

C Match the opposites.

1. formal _____   **a.** cool

2. outdated _____   **b.** expensive

3. cheap _____   **c.** fashionable, stylish

4. warm _____   **d.** heavy

5. handmade _____   **e.** casual, informal

6. light _____   **f.** machine-made

D Complete the sentences with the words in exercise **C**.

1. It's going to be cold tomorrow. You should take a _____ jacket.

2. You can't wear those _____ jeans. You should buy stylish ones.

3. _____ clothes are more expensive than machine-made clothes.

4. Looks are important, so I always wear a _____ suit when I meet clients.

Grammar: Comparatives

Comparative forms of adjectives		
Adjectives with one syllable Add -er.	cheap	Machine-made sweaters are **cheaper than** handmade sweaters.
Adjectives that end in -y Change the -y to i and add -er.	pretty	I like that dress, but this one is **prettier**.
Adjectives with two or more syllables Use more or less before the adjective.	beautiful	Eleanor is **more beautiful than** Eva.
	expensive	These suits are **less expensive than** those.
Irregular comparatives	good	Shopping in a store is **better than** shopping online.
	bad	My grades are **worse than** yours.

*The comparative form is often followed by *than*.
*Use *much* to make a comparison stronger. *This coat is **much better than** the other one.*

A Complete the sentences. Use the comparative form of the word in parentheses.

1. I prefer the green handbag, but it is _____
   (expensive) the blue purse.

2. These jeans are _____ (nice) those ones.

3. These shoes are _____ (formal) those ones.

4. This sweater is _____ (light) that one.

5. I think the blue blouse is _____ (pretty) the black one.

Conversation

A 🔊 **11** Listen to the conversation. Danny and Edris are shopping. What is Danny looking for?

Edris: Look at these blue shoes. They look nice.
Danny: I don't know. I need something more formal. They're for work.
Edris: What about these black ones?
Danny: Mmm, I'm not sure. They're a little expensive.

Edris: Look! Here are some cheaper ones.
Danny: Yes, they're very nice. Oh, they're a size 10. Do they have them in a smaller size?
Edris: Yes, here is a size 9.
Danny: Perfect.

B 🔁 Practice the conversation. Switch roles and practice it again.

C 🔁 Change *shoes* to a singular item of clothing, for example *blouse*, and practice the conversation. Don't forget to change the agreements:

*Look at **this** blue blouse. **It looks** nice.*

D **GOAL CHECK** ✓ **Make comparisons**

Write sentences comparing the clothes that you like to wear with the clothes that your parents like to wear.

Real Language

We can say *I don't know* or *I'm not sure* to show uncertainty.

I like to wear jeans. My father likes to wear a suit.

Listening

A 🔊 12 Listen. What is the woman buying?

B 🔊 12 Fill in the blanks with comparatives using the adjectives in parentheses. Listen and check your answers.

1. **Shopper:**   Do you have anything less formal?

   Sales attendant: Yes, these are _____ (casual).

2. **Shopper:**   Do you have a _____ (big) size?

   Sales attendant: How about these? Are they _____ (good)?

3. **Shopper:**   Do you have anything _____ (expensive)?

   Sales attendant: Something _____ (cheap)?

C 🔊 12 Listen again and answer the questions.

1. How many pairs of shoes does the woman try on? _____

2. How much do the white shoes cost? _____

3. How much do the black shoes cost? _____

4. What size shoes does the woman wear? _____

5. What color are the shoes that the woman buys? _____

Pronunciation: Rising and falling intonation

A 🔊 **13** Listen to the sentences. Write arrows to show rising or falling intonation.

1. Which swim suit is cheaper? The blue one or the red one?
2. Whose dress is prettier? Karen's or Mia's?
3. Which is easier? Shopping online or in a store?
4. Which do you think is warmer? The sweater or the jacket?

B 🔊 **13** Listen again. Repeat the sentences.

Communication

A Compare shopping online to shopping in a store. Write sentences using the comparatives of the adjectives.

1. safe _____
2. quick _____
3. cheap _____
4. easy _____

B 🔁 Where should these people shop—online or in a store? Compare answers with your partner and give reasons.

	Online	In store
1. Jenny needs a new dress for her birthday party tonight.		
2. Hamadi lives in a small village, a long way from the city.		
3. Kenji isn't sure which smartphone to buy.		
4. Albert is 85 years old and can't walk very far.		
5. Rosa doesn't have a credit card.		
6. Mario hates waiting in line.		

C 🔁 Discuss these questions with a partner.

1. What are the advantages and disadvantages of shopping online?
2. What are the advantages and disadvantages of shopping in a store?

D 🔁 **GOAL CHECK** ✓ **Explain preferences**

Add two more items to the list. What things do you prefer to buy online? What things do you prefer to buy in a store? Why? Share your ideas with a partner.

> I like to buy books online because it is cheaper.

> I like to buy books in a store because I can look at them.

	Online	In store
1. books		
2. clothes		
3. shoes		
4. camera		
5.		
6.		

> I really like that black leather jacket.

Language Expansion: Clothing materials

A 🔁 Take turns describing the clothes in the pictures to a partner.

100% Cotton Made in USA	100% Wool Made in Scotland	Man-made Fiber Made in Taiwan	100% Leather Made in Argentina	Pure Silk Made in China
Machine Wash, HOT Permanent Press	Hand Wash	Hand Wash	Do Not Wash	Dry-clean
Bleach as Needed	Do Not Bleach	Do Not Bleach		Do Not Bleach
Tumble Dry, MEDIUM	Dry Flat	Tumble Dry, MEDIUM		Dry Flat
Iron, Steam, or Dry, with HIGH HEAT	Iron, Steam, or Dry, with LOW HEAT	Do Not Iron		Iron, Steam or Dry, with LOW HEAT

B Read the different care instructions above. Circle **T** for *true* and **F** for *false*.

1. You can use bleach with cotton.   **T**   **F**
2. You can dry wool in a tumble dryer.   **T**   **F**
3. You have to dry-clean silk.   **T**   **F**
4. You can iron cotton.   **T**   **F**
5. You shouldn't wash leather.   **T**   **F**

Grammar: Superlatives

Superlative forms of adjectives		
Adjectives with one syllable Add *-est*.	cheap	The cotton pajamas are **the cheapest.**
Adjectives that end in -y Change the *-y* to *i* and add *-est*.	pretty	Helen is **the prettiest** girl in the class.
Adjectives with two or more syllables Use *most* or *least* before the adjective.	beautiful	These are **the most beautiful** shoes in the store.
Irregular superlatives	good	Turner's is **the best** shoe store in town.
	bad	Jon is a bad soccer player, but Tony is **the worst.**

A Complete the sentences. Use the superlative form of the adjective in parentheses.

1. These are _____ (expensive) shoes in the store.

2. Which is _____ (warm) jacket? The red one, the brown one, or the blue one?

3. Granger's Discount Store has _____ (good) prices.

4. These are _____ (formal) shoes that we have.

B Write sentences in your notebook using the pairs of adjectives in the box.

	price	weight	warmth	texture
silk	++++	+	++	++++
wool	+++	++++	++++	+
cotton	++	+++	+++	+++
man-made fiber	+	++	++	++

cheap / expensive
light / heavy
warm / cool
rough / smooth

1. *Wool is usually more expensive than cotton, but silk is the most expensive material.*

Conversation

A 🔊 **14** Listen to the conversation. Why doesn't Pablo like the leather jacket?

Pablo:	Excuse me, could you help me? I'm looking for a jacket.
Sales assistant:	Certainly, sir. I have some over here.
Pablo:	Mmm, very nice. Which is the warmest?
Sales assistant:	Well, these GORE-TEX® jackets are the warmest. They're waterproof and not too expensive.
Pablo:	No, I don't really like man-made material.
Sales assistant:	Well, we have some nice leather jackets.
Pablo:	No, I don't really like leather. It's very heavy, and I guess they are the most expensive.
Sales assistant:	Yes, they are. The cheapest is $250.

B 🔁 Practice the conversation. Switch roles and practice it again.

C 🔁 Work with a partner to make a new conversation using a different piece of clothing.

D 🔁 **GOAL CHECK** ✓ **Talk about clothing materials**

Talk with your partner. You are going on a trekking vacation and you're buying clothes. What material would you choose for the clothes in the box? Why?

hat   jacket   boots
pants   socks   shirt

Reading

A 💬 Discuss these questions with a partner.

1. What do you know about silk?
2. Where does it come from?
3. Do you have any clothes made from silk?
4. Is it cheap or expensive?

B Read the article. Answer the questions.

1. Which is the most expensive—cotton, wool, or silk? _____

2. Which country is the biggest producer of silk? _____

3. Why does Shen think that old silks are more beautiful than modern silks?

   _____

   _____

4. Why do the workers put the cocoons into hot water? _____

   _____

▲ silkworms

Word Focus

cocoon = a small bag of silk made by the silkworm

commerce = business, to make money

loom = a machine for making textiles

steel = a strong, hard metal

tomb = a place where dead people are buried

SILK
—THE QUEEN OF TEXTILES

Cotton is cool; wool is warm. They're practical. But silk? Silk is soft; it is smooth; it is sophisticated—the queen of textiles. It is also possibly the most expensive material in the world. In ancient Rome, it was more expensive than gold. But it is strong as well—a thread of silk is stronger than **steel.**

I wanted to discover more about this mysterious material, so I went to China. China is where the secret of silk was discovered more than 4,000 years ago, and it is still the biggest producer of silk in the world.

The first person I visited was Shen Congwen, advisor on ancient textiles to the Palace Museum in Beijing. He showed me some ancient silk that workers found in a **tomb** in Jianglin. It was still beautiful. He told me that he thinks old silks are more beautiful than modern silks. "In ancient times, weaving was done from the heart. In modern times, weaving is done for **commerce.**"

So, how do you make silk? The first problem is that the silkworm only eats leaves from one tree—the mulberry tree. "It is easier to prepare food for a human than a silkworm," says Toshio Ito, a Japanese silkworm expert.

Silkworms only live for about 28 days, but in that time they increase in weight 10,000 times. Then, they make a **cocoon.** Workers collect the cocoons and kill the silkworms with steam. Then, they put the cocoons into hot water to soften them. Next, they pull the fibers from the cocoon and spin them to make silk thread. Finally, they weave the thread into cloth on machines called **looms.**

But why is silk so expensive? Well, it takes 110 cocoons to make a tie, 630 cocoons to make a blouse, and 3,000 cocoons to make a kimono. That's many hours of hard work. But many people believe silk's beauty is worth it.

▲ Silk threads being woven into clothing

Writing

A Write a paragraph in your notebook about your favorite piece of clothing. Answer the questions.

- What is it made from?
- When did you get it?
- Why do you like it?
- Where did you get it?
- How much did it cost?

Communication

A 🔁 With a partner, role-play the following situation.

Student A
You are a sales assistant in a textile shop. Try to sell the handmade silk.

Student B
You are a customer. You want 5 meters of cloth for some curtains. You can spend about $200.

Types of silk	Handmade silk	Machine-made silk	Artificial silk (acetate)
Price	$55–$100 per meter	$25–$35 per meter	$15–$25 per meter

B 🔁 **GOAL CHECK** ✔ **Evaluate quality and value**

When you are buying clothes, what is most important to you? Rank the following:

_____ where it is made   _____ the price

_____ the quality   _____ the color

Compare your answers with a partner and discuss any differences.

A cotton field

Before You Watch

A Complete the passage using the words from the Word Focus box.

> 1 gallon = 3.8 liters
> 1 liter = .26 gallons

It takes about 140 liters of water to make a cup of coffee. The farmer uses water

to grow the coffee. Then water is used to (1) _____ the coffee in a factory and also to

(2) _____ the coffee to you. It also takes (3) _____ to make your

cup of coffee: gas on the farm and electricity in the factory. This puts carbon into the air, which is called a

(4) _____ . One cup of coffee puts more than 100 grams of carbon into the atmosphere.

B Guess how many liters of water it takes to produce a cotton T-shirt. Watch the video and check your guess.

    a. 700 liters   **b.** 1,700 liters   **c.** 2,700 liters

While You Watch

A ▶ Watch the video and answer the questions in your notebook.

   1. How much water does a person drink per day?

   2. List four ways your cotton T-shirt uses energy.

   3. How many gallons of water does it take to do one load of wash?

   4. How can you reduce your T-shirt's carbon footprint?

Word Focus

carbon footprint = the amount of carbon a person puts into the atmosphere

energy = power from electricity, coal, gas, etc. It makes machines work.

manufacture = to make something, usually in a factory

transport = move things from one place to another, usually by truck, boat, or airplane

After You Watch

A 👥 There are many ways to reduce your carbon footprint. You can use public transportation, ride a bicycle, or buy local vegetables. With a group, think of other ways you can reduce your carbon footprint. Share your ideas with the class.

TEDTALKS

Before You Watch

A Match the items to create complete sentences.

1. Communication is . . .   _____

2. The Internet is . . .   _____

3. The senses are . . .   _____

4. Species are . . .   _____

a. how a person or animal receives information about their environment.

b. a system of computer networks.

c. groups of animals that are similar.

d. using words, sounds, or signs to exchange information, thoughts, or feelings.

B Look at the words in the box. Choose the correct word to complete each sentence.

> **WORD BANK**
>
> **alien** a creature from outer space
> **bonobo** a rare, intelligent ape related to the chimpanzee
> **interact** to communicate with
> **interface** system linking two things
> **interplanetary** between different planets
> **interspecies** between different species
> **sentient** a being capable of experiencing the world through its senses

1. A computer has an _____ to connect to the Internet.

2. Creatures that can think are called
_____.

3. A creature from another world is called a(n)
_____.

4. People from around the world
_____ using the Internet.

5. Something that connects many planets is
_____.

> Diana Reiss, Peter Gabriel, Neil Gershenfeld, and Vint Cerf's idea worth spreading is that the Internet isn't just for humans—animals should have access too. Watch the full TED Talk at TED.com.

6. People and gorillas can communicate using _____ communication.

7. A _____ is a type of very intelligent ape.

C 🔁 Can you think of a situation where people and animals communicate, or animals communicate with other animals? Can you think of a situation where you communicate with a machine? Discuss your ideas with a partner.

D 🔁 You are going to watch a TED Talk about a new idea for an Interspecies Internet. Write down three things you think you will see in the video. Share your ideas with a partner.

While You Watch

A ▶ Watch the TED Talk. Put the images on the next page in order. Write the number in the box.

B 🔁 Write down two or three ideas from each speaker. After the TED Talk, discuss the ideas with a partner.

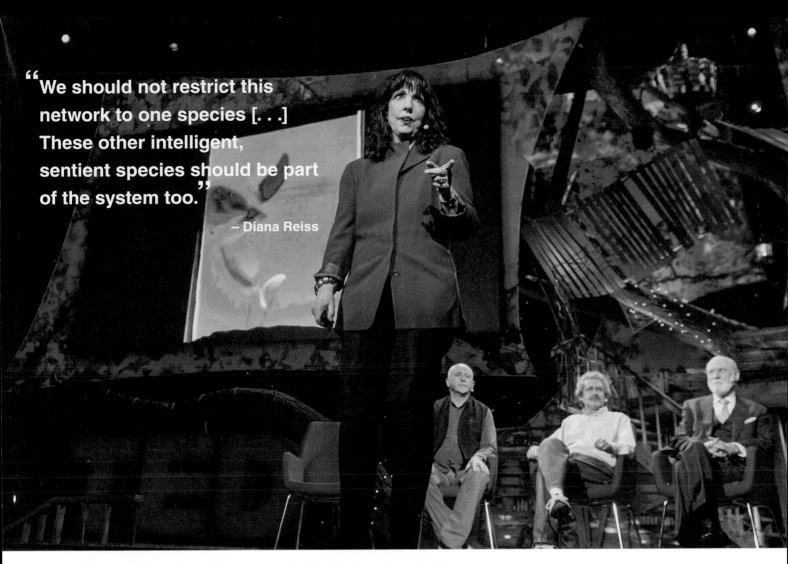

"We should not restrict this network to one species [. . .] These other intelligent, sentient species should be part of the system too."

— Diana Reiss

☐ "We thought, perhaps the most amazing tool that man's created is the Internet, and what would happen if we could somehow find new interfaces, visual-audio interfaces that would allow these remarkable sentient beings that we share the planet with access?"

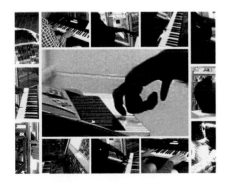

☐ "I work with a lot of musicians from around the world, and often we don't have any common language at all, but we sit down behind our instruments, and suddenly there's a way for us to connect."

☐ "We participate in the Apps for Apes program Orangutan Outreach, and we use iPads to help stimulate and enrich the animals."

☐ "Now, there is a project that's underway called the Interplanetary Internet . . . What we're learning with these interactions with other species will teach us, ultimately, how we might interact with an alien from another world."

Diana Reiss, Peter Gabriel,
Neil Gershenfeld, and Vint Cerf
THE INTERSPECIES INTERNET?
AN IDEA IN PROGRESS

After You Watch

A Watch the TED Talk again. Match each speaker with the correct description.

1. _____ Peter Gabriel

2. _____ Neil Gershenfeld

3. _____ Vint Cerf

4. _____ Diana Reiss

a. He thinks that the Interspecies Internet can also be used to communicate with life on other planets.

b. He showed how the Interspecies Internet can work by video conferencing with animals.

c. She showed that dolphins can recognize themselves.

d. He played music with a bonobo.

B Read the list of ideas presented by the TED speakers. Then work with a partner to make two predictions for each idea.

Idea	Predictions
1. communicating with other species using music	**a.** **b.**
2. the Interspecies Internet	**a.** **b.**
3. the Internet of Things	**a.** **b.**
4. the Interplanetary Internet	**a.** **b.**
5. communication with aliens	**a.** **b.**

An orangutan interacts with a tablet.

C Get together with another pair. Take turns sharing your predictions. Explain which of the outcomes you find most interesting and why. Share your ideas with the class.

D Think about how *you* communicate. Read the list of modes of communication below. Then, with a group, talk about which are the two best and worst ways to communicate with friends. Why?

e-mail	text message	in person
social media	letter	phone
letter	video conferencing	

E With your group, imagine that you are going to communicate with the following animals. How does each animal communicate? Why does each animal communicate? Do you think you would be able to communicate with each one? If so, how? Share your ideas with the class.

bonobo	elephant
dolphin	orangutan
dog	cat
parot	bee

Challenge! Diana Reiss has been doing experiments with dolphins since her first dolphin-keyboard experiment in the 1980s. Read more about her at TED.com. Find her TED Talk "Thinking Dolphin" online. With a partner, pick one more part of her work to share with the class. Do more research if needed.

Lifestyles

A fisherman stands in a wooden boat on calm water. Below his boat, baitfish shine in the waters of the Dampier Strait in Indonesia.

Look at the photo, answer the questions:

1 What does the photo show about the fisherman's lifestyle?

2 What is your lifestyle like? Can you improve it?

UNIT 10 GOALS

1. Give advice on healthy habits

2. Compare lifestyles

3. Ask about lifestyles

4. Evaluate your lifestyle

GOAL 1: Give Advice on Healthy Habits

Vocabulary

Alicia has a healthy lifestyle. She's in good shape because she works out at the gym every day. She eats healthy food, like fresh fruits and vegetables.

Robert doesn't have a good lifestyle. He's in bad shape because he never gets any exercise. He eats too much junk food, so he's overweight.

A Complete the sentences with the words in blue.

1. I need to exercise more. I'm in _____ .

2. Helen doesn't have a _____ diet. She eats a lot of junk food.

3. I have a healthy _____ . I don't smoke and I exercise regularly.

4. I need to change my diet. I eat too much _____ .

5. Jane is looking much better. She _____ and eats healthy food, like vegetables and fruit. Soon she'll be in _____ .

B Write the activities in the correct column in the chart below.

▲ cycling

▲ smoking

▲ watching lots of TV

▲ drinking lots of water

▲ getting eight hours of sleep every night

▲ sunbathing

▲ eating a balanced diet

▲ eating lots of sugar

Healthy	Unhealthy

Grammar: Modals (*could, ought to, should, must*); *have to*

Make suggestions	Give advice	Express obligation
You **could** stop smoking.	You **should/ought to** stop smoking.	You **must/have to** stop smoking.
! gentle	!! strong	!!! very strong

A Write advice for the following situations in your notebook.

1. Tell your sister to stop smoking. !!!
2. Tell your father to go on a diet. !!
3. Tell your friend to stop watching so much television. !
4. Tell your brother to get more exercise. !!
5. Tell your mother to get more sleep. !
6. Tell your friend to stop sunbathing. !!!

B Write the advice you would give to these people in your notebook. Then compare your advice with your partner's. Discuss differences.

1. Aisha wants to lose weight.
2. Yun wants to be on the Olympic swimming team.
3. Arata works too much.
4. Jaime needs some money.
5. Jack isn't happy at work.
6. Sam wants to get better grades.

Conversation

A 🔊 **15** Listen to the conversation. Why does Alex want to lose weight?

Alex: I need to lose some weight. My clothes don't fit anymore. What should I do?

Faisal: Well, instead of watching TV all day, you could get more exercise.

Alex: Like what?

Faisal: Like cycling, or you could work out at the gym.

Alex: I don't have time. I'm too busy.

Faisal: OK. Then you could change your diet. Eat something healthier, like fruit.

Alex: You mean, no more hamburgers! Oh no!

Faisal: OK. Buy some bigger clothes then.

B Practice the conversation with a partner. Switch roles and practice it again.

C **GOAL CHECK** ✔ **Give advice on healthy habits**

Ask your partner questions about the activities on page 124. Then give your partner advice.

Real Language

We use *like what?* to ask for an example. We can use *like* to give an example.

> Do you get eight hours of sleep every night?

> No, I don't.

> You should get more sleep.

▲ Ben

▲ Maggie

▲ Anita

Listening

A 👥 🔊 **16** Look at the photos. Guess who is healthy or unhealthy. Rank the people from healthy lifestyle to unhealthy lifestyle. Compare your answers with your classmates. Listen and check.

⟵ ————— ————— ————— ⟶

Healthy lifestyle   **Unhealthy lifestyle**

B 🔊 **16** Listen again and answer the questions.

1. Does Ben exercise every day? _____

2. Does Ben smoke? _____

3. What exercise does Maggie do? _____

4. Name two things that Maggie has for breakfast. _____

5. Where does Anita get her vegetables? _____

6. What is Anita's one bad habit? _____

C 🔄 Work with a partner. What advice would you give to Ben, Maggie, and Anita on how to improve their lifestyles?

Pronunciation: *Should, shouldn't*

A 🔊 **17** Listen to the sentences. Notice the difference between *should* and *shouldn't*.

I **should** get more sleep.   They **shouldn't** eat junk food.

B 🔊 **18** Listen to the conversations and circle *should* or *shouldn't*.

Conversation 1
Lorena: What can I do to improve my image?
Zuleja: Well, you (should | shouldn't) change your hairstyle. Your hair looks great!
Lorena: And what about my clothes?
Zuleja: I think you (should | shouldn't) buy some more fashionable clothes. You (should | shouldn't) wear less makeup as well.

Conversation 2
Bill: What can I do to change my image?
Adrian: I think you (should | shouldn't) shave your beard, but you (should | shouldn't) change your hairstyle.
Bill: And what about my clothes?
Adrian: You (should | shouldn't) buy some new clothes.

C 🔄 Choose one of the conversations and practice with a partner.

Fresh vegetables are part of a healthy diet.

Communication

A 👥 Answer the questions for yourself. Then survey two classmates.

Lifestyle choices	Me		Classmate 1 Name _____		Classmate 2 Name _____	
Do you play computer games?	Yes ➜ No	_____ hours per day	Yes ➜ No	_____ hours per day	Yes ➜ No	_____ hours per day
Do you eat fresh vegetables?	Yes ➜ No	_____ per day	Yes ➜ No	_____ per day	Yes ➜ No	_____ per day
Do you spend time on social media?	Yes ➜ No	_____ hours per day	Yes ➜ No	_____ hours per day	Yes ➜ No	_____ hours per day
Do you work out every day?	Yes ➜ No	_____ hours per day	Yes ➜ No	_____ hours per day	Yes ➜ No	_____ hours per day
Do you drink coffee or tea every day?	Yes ➜ No	_____ cups per day	Yes ➜ No	_____ cups per day	Yes ➜ No	_____ cups per day
Do you eat sugary foods?	Yes ➜ No	_____ per day	Yes ➜ No	_____ per day	Yes ➜ No	_____ per day

B 🔄 Tell a partner about you and the classmates you interviewed.

C 👥 Tell your group about your lifestyle.

> Ramona and I never play computer games, but Alfredo plays for about two hours per day.

D 👥 **GOAL CHECK** ✓ **Compare lifestyles**

As a group, decide who has the best lifestyle and give reasons.

> Salma works out in the gym every day for two hours and doesn't eat sugary foods.

> Yahir eats five pieces of sugary food per day and never works out. Salma has a much better lifestyle.

stress-free

Language Expansion: Compound adjectives

A Match the compound adjectives to their meanings.

a. works too much
b. delicious
c. without worries or problems
d. not high in calories
e. makes you happy
f. produced in your own garden
g. all your life
h. not made in a factory

1. mouth-watering _____
2. homemade _____
3. heartwarming _____
4. lifelong _____

5. stress-free _____
6. homegrown _____
7. overworked _____
8. low-calorie _____

B Complete the sentences. Use adjectives from exercise **A**.

1. Kevin and I went to kindergarten together. We are _____ friends.

2. When I was a child, my father had a vegetable garden, so we ate lots of _____ fruit and vegetables.

3. I have to work long hours, and I'm always tired. I think I am _____.

4. My grandmother makes the best _____ chicken soup in the world! It's absolutely _____.

Grammar: Questions with *how*

How much exercise do you get?	**How long** did your grandfather live?
How many cigarettes do you smoke a day?	**How often** do you go to the gym?
How old is your father?	

*We use **how much** to ask about the quantity of non-countable nouns.
*We use **how many** to ask about the quantity of countable nouns.
*We use **how old** to ask about age.
*We use **how long** to ask about length or a period of time.
*We use **how often** to ask about frequency.

A Match the questions and the answers.

1. How often does Mike go swimming? _____
2. How old is Akuru's grandmother? _____
3. How much junk food do you eat? _____
4. How long do you think you will live? _____
5. How many cigarettes does Mario smoke a day? _____

a. She's about 95.
b. Until I'm 80.
c. About 15.
d. Not much.
e. Once a week.

B Write the questions.

Questions	Answers
1. _____	We go to the gym three times a week.
2. _____	I am 27 years old.
3. _____	I think it will take about two hours.
4. _____	I weigh 168 pounds.

C Write five *Wh-* questions in your notebook. Ask your partner the questions.

Conversation

A ◀))) 19 Listen to the conversation. What's the problem with Mr. Lopez?

Doctor:	Good morning, Mr. Lopez. How can I help you?
Mr. Lopez:	Hello, doctor. <u>I'm always tired, but when I go to bed I can't sleep</u>.
Doctor:	OK. How long have you had this problem?
Mr. Lopez:	Since I started my new job.
Doctor:	What do you do?
Mr. Lopez:	I'm in advertising.
Doctor:	How many hours do you work?
Mr. Lopez:	I work about 80 hours a week.
Doctor:	80 hours! That's a lot. And how much exercise do you get?
Mr. Lopez:	Not much. I don't have the time.
Doctor:	OK. It seems to me that you are overworked. You need to work less and find time to get more exercise. Maybe you should look for a more stress-free job.

B Practice the conversation with a partner. Switch roles and practice it again.

C Change the underlined problem to create and practice a new conversation.

D **GOAL CHECK** ✔ **Ask about lifestyles**

Ask a partner about his or her lifestyle.

Reading

A 🔁 Discuss the questions with a partner.

1. Do you want to live to be 100 years old?

2. What do you think you should do to live to be 100 years old?

B Answer the questions.

1. A long, healthy life depends on mainly two things. What are they? _____
   _____

2. Why do men live longer in Sardinia than in the United States? _____
   _____

3. How old was Ushi the last time the writer visited her? _____
   _____

4. How often should you exercise? _____
   _____

5. What are the advantages of growing your own vegetables? _____
   _____

Word Focus

genes = parts of the body that determine physical characteristics

joke = to say something that is not serious

perfume = liquid that smells good

prevent = to avoid

run away = to leave

Sardinia, Italy and Okinawa, Japan

THE SECRETS OF LONG LIFE

A long, healthy life is no accident. It begins with good **genes,** but it also depends on good habits. If you have a healthy lifestyle, experts say you may live up to ten years longer. So what is the secret of a long life?

I visited places in the world where many people live to be 100 years old, including Sardinia in Italy and Okinawa in Japan. Sardinians and Okinawans live longer, have fewer illnesses, and enjoy long, healthy lives.

SARDINIANS

First, I went to Sardinia, where many people, especially men, live longer than in other parts of the world. Generally, women live longer than men. In fact, in America, there are four times as many 100-year-old women as men. However, in Sardinia, an equal number of men and women reach 100.

The reason is possibly that the men have a stress-free life working outside, while the women look after the house and the family money. "I do the work," says Tonino, holding his wife Giovanna around the waist. "My wife does the worrying."

OKINAWANS

Since I last visited Ushi five years ago, she's taken a new job, tried to **run away** from home, and started wearing **perfume.** Normal for a young woman, perhaps, but Ushi is 103. When I ask about the perfume, she **jokes** that she has a new boyfriend, then puts a hand over her mouth and laughs.

"Okinawans have one-fifth the heart disease, one-fourth the breast and prostate cancer, and one-third less mental health problems than Americans,"

says Craig Willcox of the Okinawa Centenarian Study. What's the key to their success? "*Ikigai* certainly helps," Willcox says. The word translates to "reason for living," and it may help to prevent stress and diseases such as high blood pressure.

Okinawans have a low-calorie diet. "A full plate of Okinawan vegetables, tofu, miso soup, and a little fish or meat contains fewer calories than a small hamburger," says Makoto Suzuki of the Okinawa Centenarian Study. "And it will have many more healthy nutrients."

When she's not watching sumo wrestling on TV, Yasu Itoman, 100, gets her own exercise by growing onions, tomatoes, carrots, and other herbs and vegetables in her garden. Her homegrown vegetables may help **prevent** cancer.

Bosa, Sardinia

Do you play a sport?

Yes, I do.

What sport do you play?

Communication

A Go around the class and find someone who does each of the following. Write the names in the chart, and then ask a follow-up question.

Find someone who . . .	Name
1. . . . plays a sport.	
2. . . . has a stress-free life.	
3. . . . has a clear reason for living.	
4. . . . grows his or her own vegetables.	
5. . . . has a grandparent more than 70 years old.	

Min-jun plays football.

Seo-yeon has a stress-free life. She does yoga.

B Report to the class.

Writing

A Write a paragraph about your own lifestyle. Answer the questions.

1. Do you lead a healthy lifestyle?

2. How often do you exercise?

3. What sort of food do you eat?

4. Do you get enough sleep?

5. How can you improve your lifestyle?

B **GOAL CHECK** ✔ **Evaluate your lifestyle**

Discuss with a partner the good habits and the bad habits in your lifestyles. Take turns. Give each other advice.

Traffic can be very stressful.

Before You Watch

A Make a list of things that can cause stress. Discuss your list with a partner.

B Match the words and the definitions.

1. hormones _____
2. physical stress _____
3. mental stress _____

a. stress on your body, like running
b. stress on your mind, like too much work
c. chemicals produced by your body

Word Focus

If you feel under **stress**, you feel worried and tense because of difficulties in your life.

While You Watch

A Watch the video. Circle **T** for *true* and **F** for *false*.

1. There are two types of stress: physical and mental. **T** **F**
2. Stress produces hormones. **T** **F**
3. When you exercise, you don't burn all the hormones. **T** **F**
4. Long-term hormones can cause problems. **T** **F**

After You Watch

A Discuss the questions with a partner.

1. What did you learn from this video?
2. Will it change your lifestyle?

Communication

A Work in groups of three or four. You have been assigned to design your school's or office's Anti-Stress Campaign. Make a list of four things you will do.

Achievements

A single climber **stands on a peak above** the clouds in Greenland.

UNIT 11 GOALS

1. Talk about today's chores

2. Interview for a job

3. Talk about personal accomplishments

4. Discuss humanity's greatest achievements

GOAL 1: Talk About Today's Chores

pay the bills
buy the groceries
sweep the floor
cut the grass
walk the dog
vacuum
iron the clothes
put away the clothes

Word Focus

chore = A *chore* is a task that must be done, but that many people find boring or unpleasant.

Vocabulary

A Label the pictures with phrases from the box.

1. _____ 2. _____ 3. _____ 4. _____

5. _____ 6. _____ 7. _____ 8. _____

B In your notebook, write down which chores from exercise **A** you think are easy and which chores you think are difficult.

C In your family, who does the household chores? Discuss with a partner.

Grammar: Present perfect tense

Present perfect tense	
Statement	He **has ironed** the clothes.
Negative	I **haven't cooked** lunch yet.
Yes/No questions	**Have you finished** your homework?
Short answers	Yes, I **have.**/No, I **haven't.**
Wh- questions	What **have you done** today?

*The present perfect tense is formed with the verb *has/have* + the past participle of the verb.
*We use the present perfect tense to talk about an event that started in the past and continues in the present: *I have lived here all my life,* or an event that was completed at an unspecified time in the past: *I have read the book.*

*Some verbs have regular past participles. They end in *-ed.*		*Some verbs have irregular past participles.	
pass – passed	graduate – graduated	have – had	take – taken
clean – cleaned	travel – traveled	go – gone	pay – paid
iron – ironed	visit – visited	be – been	put – put

A Write the irregular past participles from the box next to the correct verb.

1. buy _____
2. do _____
3. drink _____
4. eat _____

5. make _____
6. meet _____
7. read _____
8. say _____

9. speak _____
10. sweep _____
11. tell _____
12. win _____

read   spoken   drunk
bought   swept   told
won   said   made
eaten   met   done

B Complete the conversation with the present perfect tense.

1. **A:** What (1) _____ (you, do) today?

   B: Nothing very exciting. I (2) _____ (clean) the house, and I (3) _____ (cook) dinner. (4) _____ (you, have) an interesting day?

   A: No, not really. (5) _____ (I, be) sick. I (6) _____ (not do) anything.

2. **A:** Today, I (1) _____ (pay the bills) and I (2) _____ (buy the groceries). (3) _____ (you, have) an interesting day?

   B: Well, I (4) _____ (visit) a friend. Then, I (5) _____ (buy) some clothes for my new job.

C Ask your partner questions using the present perfect.

Conversation

A ◀))20 Read the Real Language box and listen to the conversation. Has Lynn done her chores?

Mom: Hi, honey. I'm home.
Lynn: Hi, Mom.
Mom: Have you <u>walked the dog</u>?
Lynn: Yes, Mom. Of course I've walked the dog. And I've <u>vacuumed the living room</u>.
Mom: And <u>have you done your homework</u>?
Lynn: Mom! I've been busy <u>walking the dog</u> and <u>vacuuming</u>. I haven't had time.
Mom: Sorry, honey. It's just I've had a long day myself.

B Practice the conversation with a partner. Switch roles and practice it again.

C Replace the underlined chores and practice the conversation again.

D **GOAL CHECK** ✔ **Talk about today's chores**

Talk to a partner about the chores you have done this week.

Have you paid your electric bill this month?

Real Language

We use *of course* to show something is obvious.

Achievements   137

B GOAL 2: Interview for a Job

Mesa Verde, Colorado, USA

NEEDED URGENTLY!

TOUR GUIDE
Mesa Verde
Professional appearance. Good interpersonal skills. Experience an advantage. Driver's license essential. Call 2356 9845.

Yuki

Richard

Listening

A 21 Read the ad. Listen to Richard and Yuki at the interview. Use the boxes to take notes on their qualifications.

B 21 The interviewers asked the following questions. Complete the questions. Listen again to check your answers.

1. Have you ____________________ from college?
2. Have you ever ____________________ as a tour guide?
3. Who is the most interesting person you have ever ____________________?
4. Have you ____________________ your driving test?

C Answer the questions.

1. Has Richard ever traveled abroad? ____________________
2. How many countries has Yuki visited? ____________________
3. Who is the most interesting person Yuki has met? ____________________
4. Has Richard passed his driving test? ____________________
5. Has Yuki graduated from college? ____________________

D Who should get the job? Discuss with a partner.

Pronunciation: Reduced form of *have*

A 🔊)22 Listen to the examples. Notice the pronunciation of the reduced forms.

Full form	Reduced form
I have	I've
have you	/hæv-jə/
you have	you've
has he	/hæz-i/
she has	she's

B 🔊)23 Listen to the sentences. Check (✓) the correct column.

	Full form	Reduced form
1. Has she left?		
2. Have you finished?		
3. Has he read this book?		
4. Have you done your homework?		
5. I have never been to the USA.		

C 🔊)23 Listen again. Repeat the sentences.

Communication

A 🔁 Read the following ads. Then role-play an interview. For the first ad, **Student A** is the interviewer and **Student B** is the interviewee. Change roles for the second ad. When you are the interviewee, you can be yourself or pretend to be someone interested in the job.

```
========= WANTED! =========

┌─────────────────────────────┐
│  Handyman for Kindergarten  │
└─────────────────────────────┘

Small kindergarten needs a person
to help with maintenance—
plumbing, carpentry, fixing our
vehicles, etc. No experience with
children necessary but must enjoy
being around kids. Any age. $25 per
hour.
```

```
┌─────────────────────────────┐
│          LIFEGUARD          │
└─────────────────────────────┘

18–30 yrs old. You must be in very
good shape. Must be able to
swim 250 meters in 4 minutes and
run 2,000 meters in 10 minutes.
Experience an advantage. Some
training offered.

Flexible hours.
```

B 🔁 **GOAL CHECK** ✓ **Interview for a job**

Think of another job. What is required? Write notes. Interview a partner. Switch roles and repeat.

get a promotion
travel abroad
pass your driving test
run a marathon
get a credit card
graduate from high
school/college

Word Focus

accomplishment = something
remarkable that a person has
done

Language Expansion: Personal accomplishments

A Label the pictures with phrases from the box.

1. _____ 2. _____ 3. _____

4. _____ 5. _____ 6. _____

B Check (✓) the achievements in exercise **A** that you have done.

C 🔁 Ask a partner what he or she has achieved. Take turns.

**Have you passed
your driving test?**

Grammar: Present perfect tense vs. simple past tense

Present perfect tense vs. simple past tense	
The present perfect tense is used to show an action that happened at any time in the past.	The simple past tense is used to show an action that happened at a specific time in the past.
*Claudio **has been** to many countries.*	*He **went** to France last year.*

*We often use time expressions with the simple past tense, for example, *yesterday, last week, in 2010.*
*We use expressions like *just, never, ever, yet* with the present perfect tense.
  *Have you **ever** been to another country?*
  *Nayla has **just** returned from France.*
  *I have **never** been there.*
  *I haven't graduated **yet**.*

Past   Simple past tense   Now   Future
              ↓

Present perfect tense

A Complete the sentences with the correct form of the verb in parentheses.

1. Last summer, we _____ (go) to the Maldives.

2. I _____ (live) in the same house all my life.

3. John _____ (never travel) abroad.

4. Spain _____ (win) the World Cup in 2010.

5. Brazil _____ (win) the World Cup five times.

B Complete the conversations with the correct form of the verb in parentheses.

1. **A:** _____ (you pass) your driving test?

   B: Yes. I _____ (take) it in January, and I

   _____ (pass) the first time.

2. **A:** _____ (you be) to Europe?

   B: Yes, I have. I _____ (go) to Germany last year.

Conversation

A 🔊24 Listen to the conversation. Who has started his own business?

Alfredo: Hi, Pete. I haven't seen you for a long time. What's new?

Pete: Lots! I quit my job with <u>CompuSoft</u>, and I've started <u>my own computer business</u>.

Alfredo: Congratulations! When did you <u>open the business</u>?

Pete: Eight months ago, and it's going well.

Alfredo: Great!

Pete: And what about you?

Alfredo: Things haven't changed much. I'm still <u>working at the bank</u>. But I've <u>bought a new house</u>. It's right next to Central Park.

Pete: Wow! Nice area.

Alfredo: Yeah. You should come 'round and visit some time.

Pete: Will do, when I have some time.

B 🔁 Practice the conversation with a partner. Switch roles and practice it again.

C 🔁 Change the underlined words and practice the conversation again.

D 🔁 **GOAL CHECK** ✔ **Talk about personal accomplishments**

Talk to a partner about your personal accomplishments or what you would like to achieve in the future.

Reading

A What do you think are humanity's greatest achievements? Discuss with a partner.

B Read the article. Circle all the verbs in the present perfect tense.

C Read the article. Circle **T** for *true* or **F** for *false*.

1. Humanity has lived on Earth for a long time. **T F**

2. Many of humanity's greatest achievements are in science and technology. **T F**

3. Antibiotics are machines. **T F**

4. Art makes people happy. **T F**

5. Humanity started to use fire a long time ago. **T F**

D Answer the questions. Give your own opinions. Share your answers with a group.

1. Imagine life without electricity. How would it be different?

2. Many achievements have a negative effect. What are the negative effects of cars?

3. Do you think the Mona Lisa is a great achievement?

4. How would you define "great"?

Word Focus

antibiotic = a medicine that kills bacteria. Penicillin is an antibiotic.

printing press = a machine that prints books

The Louvre, Paris, France

HUMANITY'S GREATEST ACHIEVEMENTS

The Earth is 4.5 billion years old, but the human race has lived on it for just 200,000 years. In that short time, we have achieved some incredible things.

Many of humanity's great achievements are in science and technology. The list is almost endless. The invention of the airplane has changed our lives. The discovery of **antibiotics** has saved the lives of millions of people. Can you imagine living without electricity? What about the **printing press?** Without the printing press, you wouldn't be reading this. In the last 50 years, there have been astonishing achievements in communication, such as radio, TV, computers, the Internet, and smartphones. Could we live without these things? Probably, but would life be as interesting?

What about the arts? The arts have brought pleasure to many people, but are the Beatles and Bach more important than antibiotics? And is the *Mona Lisa* as important an achievement as going to space?

Finally, we must not forget humanity's early achievements, like the use of fire for cooking and heating, and the invention of the wheel. Can you imagine modern life without cooked food and cars?

What are humanity's greatest achievements? To answer the question, we need to decide what we mean by "great." Is it something that makes us rich or happy or saves lives? Or is it just something that makes us say "Wow," like the Pyramids of Giza? What do you think?

The Great Pyramids of Giza, Egypt

GOAL 4: Discuss Humanity's Greatest Achievements

An astronaut on the moon

▲ The *Mona Lisa*

Communication

A Here is a list of five important human achievements. Rank them in order of importance.

_____ the use of fire

_____ walking on the moon

_____ the Internet

_____ electricity

_____ antibiotics

_____ art

B 🗣 Compare your list with a partner. Talk about your differences.

C 👥 Join another pair and compare your lists.

Writing

A Choose one important human achievement. It can be **any** achievement, not just from the reading. Write what you know about it, and say why you think it is an important achievement.

B 🗣 **GOAL CHECK** ✔ **Discuss humanity's greatest achievements**

Talk with a partner about the achievements you wrote about. Ask and answer questions about the achievements you chose.

Before You Watch

A Read the summary of the video and fill in the blanks with words from the box. Then watch the video and check your answers.

weightless   survive
underwater   oxygen
solar panels

Video summary

In space, there is no _____ . It is impossible to breathe. Sometimes astronauts have to make a

spacewalk outside the spacecraft. In order to _____ , astronauts wear special space suits. They do

jobs like repair _____ . It is dangerous work.

They prepare for their spacewalks _____ in special tanks. It is like being _____
in space but much safer.

While You Watch

A ▶ Watch the video and circle **T** for *true* or **F** for *false*.

1. It is always very cold in space.   **T   F**

2. Space suits are filled with oxygen.   **T   F**

3. The first person to walk in space was
   Edward White.   **T   F**

4. Astronauts fixed the solar panels
   on the Hubble Space Telescope.   **T   F**

After You Watch

A 🔁 Scientific achievements can be expensive. The National Aeronautics
and Space Administration (NASA) spent almost $18 billion in 2014. The
Large Hadron Collider (a huge scientific instrument), cost $4.6 billion.
Discuss these questions with a partner. Why do people spend a lot of money
on big science projects? Is it worth it?

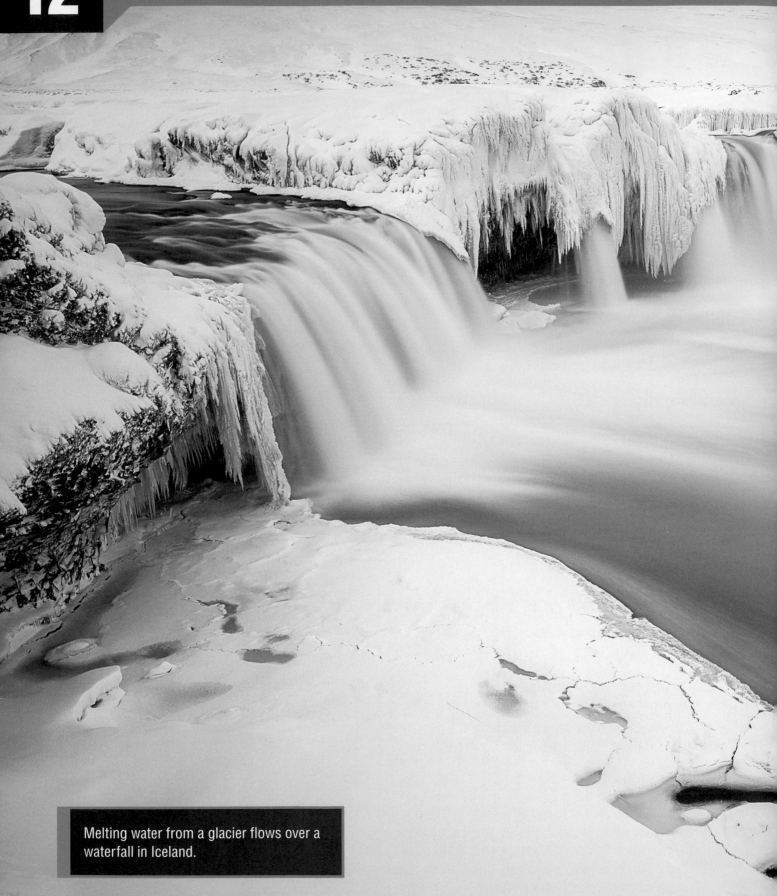

Melting water from a glacier flows over a waterfall in Iceland.

Look at the photo, answer the questions:

1 What does this photo show?

2 What is the cause and effect demonstrated by this photo?

UNIT 12 GOALS

1. Talk about managing your money

2. Make choices on how to spend your money

3. Talk about cause and effect

4. Evaluate money and happiness

Vocabulary

A Read the article from a student magazine.

STUDENT LIFE

MANAGE YOUR MONEY

Congratulations! You have received your first **student loan**. How are you going to spend it? Are you going to go out and buy that new cell phone or those cool sneakers? Well, don't!

Before you spend a penny, you have to make a **budget** and plan your spending. First, write down your **income**—how much money you receive. Then calculate your **expenses** (rent, transportation, food). If your expenses are lower than your income

you are on the right track! Now you know how much money you have left to spend each month. But don't **overspend** or you will have to **borrow** money. Borrowing money from the bank is expensive. **Interest rates** are high. You could check to see if a friend or family member can **lend** you the money.

You also have to think about the long term. How are you going to pay for that spring break at the beach, or buy your family presents? You will have to **save** some money every month. So, that new cell phone can wait. Manage your money and maybe you'll be able to take that spring break at the beach—in Mexico!

21

Word Focus

student loan = money that the government lends to students

B Write the words in blue next to the correct meanings.

1. the amount of money you spend _____

2. to ask someone to give you money _____

3. the amount of money you receive _____

4. to spend too much money _____

5. a spending plan _____

6. to give someone money _____

7. to put money in the bank for the future _____

8. the percentage (%) charged when you borrow money _____

Grammar: Real conditionals (or first conditional)

If clause (simple present tense)	Result clause (future tense)
If I **buy** a new TV,	I **will** not **have** enough money to pay the rent.
If they **borrow** some money,	they **will be able to** buy a new house.
We use real conditional sentences to express possible results of choices we make. *When the *if* clause comes first, there is a comma between the *if* clause and the result clause.*	

A Match the *if* clauses to the correct result clauses.

1. If you borrow money from the bank, _____
2. If you save some money every month, _____
3. If you lend money to your sister, _____
4. If your expenses are bigger than your income, _____
5. If we eat at home instead of in a restaurant, _____

a. she won't return the money until the end of the month.
b. you won't have enough money to pay the rent.
c. we will have enough money to go to the theater.
d. the interest rates will be high.
e. you will have enough money to buy a new computer.

B Unscramble the words to write conditional sentences. Don't forget the punctuation.

1. a bigger car   some money   we borrow   If   we can buy
   If we borrow some money, we can buy a bigger car.

2. a new job   more money   I will have   I get   If
   _____

3. on vacation   we overspend   If   to go   we won't be able
   _____

4. you won't have to   I   use your credit card   If   lend you $100
   _____

5. our car   sell   we will be able to rent   If we   a bigger apartment
   _____

Conversation

A 🔊 **25** Listen to the conversation. What choice does Jim have to make?

Jim: I don't know what to do. I want to take a vacation, and I also want to buy a new camera.
Dave: I see. If you buy the camera, you won't have enough money for the vacation. Is that it?
Jim: You got it.
Dave: So, just take the vacation. Don't buy the camera.
Jim: But if I don't buy the camera, I won't be able to take any vacation photos.
Dave: OK, just buy the camera.
Jim: But if I buy the camera, I won't be able to take the vacation, and I won't need a camera.
Dave: Hmm . . . you have a problem.

> **Real Language**
>
> *to get* sometimes means *to understand*
> (Do you) get it? = Do you understand?
> You got it! = You understood.
> I don't get you/it. = I don't understand you/it.

B 🔄 Practice the conversation with a partner. Switch roles and practice it again.

C 🔄 Use the words in the box to make a new conversation.

D 🔄 **GOAL CHECK** ✔ **Talk about managing your money**

Work with a partner. Discuss how you manage your money. What are your expenses? Do you have a budget? Do you save?

> binoculars   bird watching
> weekend   glasses
> movies   bicycle
> cycling tour

B | GOAL 2: Make Choices on How to Spend Your Money

London, England

Listening

A 🔊 **26** Listen to the conversation. Circle the correct answer.

The travel agent is in _____ .

a. London   **b.** Paris   **c.** New York

B 🔊 **26** Listen again and answer the questions.

1. Is this the first time that the woman has visited England? _____

2. Why doesn't she want to take the plane? _____

3. Why doesn't she want to rent a car? _____

4. How long does it take to go from Paris to London by train? _____

5. How much does the train ticket cost? _____

Pronunciation: Intonation

A 🔊 **27** Listen to the sentences. Draw the arrows to show rise or fall.

1. If I buy a car, I won't be able to pay the rent.

2. If you take the bus, it will be cheaper.

3. If we borrow some money, we will repay it in a month.

4. If Sara leaves now, she will catch the seven o'clock train.

5. If we take the plane, it will be quicker.

B 🔊 **27** Listen again and repeat the sentences.

Communication

A  Work with a partner. Plan a six-day visit to California. Each of you has $300 to spend on transportation. You will arrive in Los Angeles. You would like to visit Yosemite National Park, San Diego, and San Francisco.

> If we take the train, will it be cheaper?

> If we take the plane, it will be quicker.

> If we take the bus, it will be cheaper.

	San Diego	San Francisco	Merced (for Yosemite)
Los Angeles	🚌 $40, 4 hours 🚆 $80, 3 hours ✈ $130, 1 hour	🚌 $60, 6 hours 🚆 $70, 8 hours (3 changes) ✈ $130, 1½ hours	🚌 $80, 7 hours 🚆 No service ✈ No service
San Diego		🚌 $135 return, 12 hours 🚆 No service ✈ $250, 1½ hours	🚌 $90, 10 hours 🚆 No service ✈ No service
San Francisco			🚌 $70, 4 hours 🚆 $60, 3 hours ✈ No service

Yosemite National Park

	Itinerary	Transportation	Transportation costs
Day 1			
Day 2			
Day 3			
Day 4			
Day 5			
Day 6			

B 🔅 **GOAL CHECK** ✔ **Make choices on how to spend your money**

Join another pair of students and explain to them how you decided to spend your transportation money.

Language Expansion: Animal habitats

A 🔁 Take turns. Make statements about animals and their **habitats**.

 ▲ desert

 ▲ mountains

 ▲ grasslands

 ▲ rain forest

 ▲ coral reef

 ▲ monkey

 ▲ camel

 ▲ shark

 ▲ mountain goat

 ▲ elephant

Word Focus

habitat = the place where a plant or animal normally lives

B Complete the sentences. Use the habitats and animals in exercise **A.**

1. Many countries near the equator have _____. They contain hundreds of different plants and animals, for example _____ and colorful birds.

2. _____ can live without water for many days. They are perfectly adapted to live in the _____.

3. The Great Barrier Reef in Australia is the biggest _____ in the world. It is the home of _____ and many other kinds of fish.

4. Kenya is famous for its _____. Tourists come from all over the world to see the animals, like lions and _____.

5. The highest _____ in the world are in Nepal. Not many animals live there. If you are lucky, you might see a _____.

Grammar: Real conditionals

Result clause (future tense)	*If* clause (simple present tense)
The climate **will** change	if we **continue** to burn fossil fuels.
We **will** lose many valuable animals	if we **destroy** their habitats.
*Real conditionals can be written with the result clause first. *These conditionals do not need a comma.	

A Use these cues to write conditional sentences.

1. children   suffer   if   don't take care of   animal habitats

   Our children will suffer if we don't take care of animal habitats.

2. fish   die   if   coral reef   die

   _____

3. visitors   not come   if   no   animals

   _____

4. live longer   if   exercise more

   _____

5. go   beach   if   no   rain

   _____

▲ Habitat destruction in a rain forest. Why is it important to save habitats like this?

B Complete the sentences using your own words.

1. Our coral reefs will die if _____.

2. We will lose many useful plants if _____.

3. _____ if you finish your work today.

4. _____ if more people use public transportation.

5. _____ if you cook dinner.

Conversation

A 🔊 **28** Listen to the conversation. What is Aya worried about? How can she help?

Aya: I'm very worried about all we hear and read about habitat destruction. It's important, but how can I help?

Sharon: You go to work by car, right?

Aya: Yes.

Sharon: It will help if you go to work by bus.

Aya: How will that help?

Sharon: Buses carry lots of people. That means less gasoline is used per person. Less pollution, less climate change, less habitat destruction, right?

Aya: Yes, and I save money as well.

Sharon: Right!

Real Language

You can say *right?* (rising tone) at the end of a statement to check information. You can also use *right* (falling tone) to show you agree.

B 🔁 Practice the conversation with a partner. Switch roles and practice it again.

C 🔁 **GOAL CHECK** ✔ **Talk about cause and effect**

Work with a partner. Choose an important problem or environmental issue. Make a list of the things you can do to help. Tell your partner what positive consequences your actions will have.

GOAL 4: Evaluate Money and Happiness

Reading

A Read the list below. Make a check mark (✓) next to the items that describe spending money.

1. _____ buying clothes for yourself

2. _____ spending time with a friend

3. _____ reading a book

4. _____ buying a present for someone in your family

5. _____ donating to a charity

6. _____ going out to eat

B 👥 In a small group, take turns saying how you would feel after doing each of the things in exercise **A.** For the situations that deal with money, which would make you feel best? Why?

C Read the article. All the following statements are false. Correct the false information in your notebook. Write the correct sentences.

1. Many people believe that winning the lottery will not make them happy.

2. People that win the lottery never have problems with money.

3. Michael Norton has done experiments to test how people feel after exercising.

4. Michael Norton's experiments show that spending money does not make people happy.

WORD BANK

conflict problem
debt money that has to be paid
experiment test
lottery game of chance with cash prize
research exploration, investigation

TED Ideas worth spreading

Michael Norton Professor/Psychologist

HOW TO BUY HAPPINESS

The following article is about Michael Norton. After Unit 12, you'll have the opportunity to watch some of Norton's TED Talk and learn more about his idea worth spreading.

Michael Norton is a business school professor. He is interested in the effects of money on how people feel.

Some people believe that having a lot of money will make them happy. For example, many people think that if they win the **lottery,** they will be happy. However, many lottery winners overspend and have many **debts.** Also, they have **conflicts** because their friends and family want gifts of money, or loans. Debts and conflicts make people unhappy. This example about lottery winners shows that, "money can't buy happiness." But is that always true?

Norton believes that money *can* buy happiness. Why? He has done **experiments** on how people behave with money. In one experiment, some university students spent money on themselves and some students spent money on other people. Afterward, all the students were asked about their feelings. The students that spent money on themselves did not feel unhappy, but they did not feel happier, either. However, the **research** shows that students that spent money on others felt happier. Michael Norton did this type of money experiment all over the world, with people of all ages. Each time, the result was the same—spending money on others improved the happiness of the giver.

How you spend your money has an effect on your happiness.

"Maybe the reason that money doesn't make us happy is that we're always spending it on the wrong things."

— Michael Norton

Writing

A A friend sent you this e-mail. Complete the e-mail.

I have some great news! I found some money on the street today. My sister's birthday is next week and I know she wants a scarf. Also, I want to buy myself some new music.

If I buy the music, I _____ not have enough money to buy the scarf. And if I _____ the money on music, I will not be able to buy the scarf. What do you think I should do?

Samuel

B Write a reply to Samuel's e-mail using information from the article. Use real conditionals to talk about the effects of Samuel's choice.

Communication

A You won $100 in the lottery. Write down five possible ways to use the money.

B 🔁 Discuss your ideas with a partner. Talk about each way to use money and discuss any differences.

C 🔁 **GOAL CHECK** ✓ **Evaluate money and happiness**

Work together to decide how to use the money. How much will you spend and what will you buy? Will you save or give away any of the money? What might happen as a result of how you spend the money?

Mount Kilimanjaro

Before You Watch

A Read the chain of actions and consequences. Number the sentences below to make a similar chain.

Cars and airplanes produce carbon dioxide. > Carbon dioxide makes the atmosphere hotter. > The glaciers of Kilimanjaro melt.

_____ Kilimanjaro's glaciers get smaller.   1 People cut down trees.

_____ There is less water in the atmosphere.   _____ There is less rain and snow.

While You Watch

A ▶ Watch the video. Fill in the numbers and dates.

1. Kilimanjaro is nearly _____ miles high.

2. It is around _____ miles south of the equator.

3. The glaciers on Kilimanjaro are _____ years old.

4. Experts think that the glaciers could disappear by the year _____.

> **Word Focus**
>
> **deforestation =** when trees and forests are cut down
>
> **glacier =** a large body of slowly moving ice
>
> **to melt =** to change from ice to water

B ▶ Watch again. Answer the questions.

1. Why are the glaciers of Kilimanjaro important to the people of Tanzania?

_____

_____

2. Why are the glaciers disappearing? _____

_____

After You Watch

A 🗘 Discuss this question with a partner: Is there anything that *you* can do to stop the melting of Kilimanjaro's glaciers?

TEDTALKS

Michael Norton Professor/Psychologist
HOW TO BUY HAPPINESS

Before You Watch

A Read the list. Make a check (✓) next to the ways that you use money.

☐ pay bills

☐ buy things for yourself

☐ save money

☐ eat at a restaurant

☐ buy gifts for others

☐ spend money on expenses

☐ donate (give away) money

☐ lend money to others

B Read the sentences. Match the word in **bold** to its meaning.

a. give someone a reason to do something	**d.** helps others
	e. money spent for a future reward
b. good effect	**f.** scientific test
c. payment that is received	**g.** how well you work

1. If I don't sleep enough, I don't **perform** well at school. _____

2. I like to get good grades in school; it **motivates** me to study. _____

3. Alexandra decided to make an **investment** with her extra money. _____

4. The **return** on the investment was small, only 20 dollars. _____

5. Jack is working on an **experiment** about sunlight. _____

6. Exercise has many **benefits**, such as being healthy. _____

7. Being a volunteer is a **prosocial** activity. _____

Michael Norton's idea worth spreading is that money *can* buy happiness! What matters isn't how much you have, but how you spend it. Watch Norton's full TED Talk on TED.com.

C 🗘 You are going to watch a TED Talk about Michael Norton's experiments on how money makes people feel. What types of experiments do you think you will see? Talk about your ideas with a partner. Look at the list in exercise **A** for ideas.

While You Watch

A ▶ Watch the TED Talk. Complete the missing information in the chart as you watch.

Experiment	How much money	Spent money on themselves	Spent money on others
	5 or _____ dollars	did not feel happier	
sales teams			sold more
dodgeball teams	did not say		won more games

B 🎲 Read the photo captions on the next page. What quotes are you surprised by? Place a check (✓) next to the captions that you are surprised by. Then, in small groups, talk about why you are surprised.

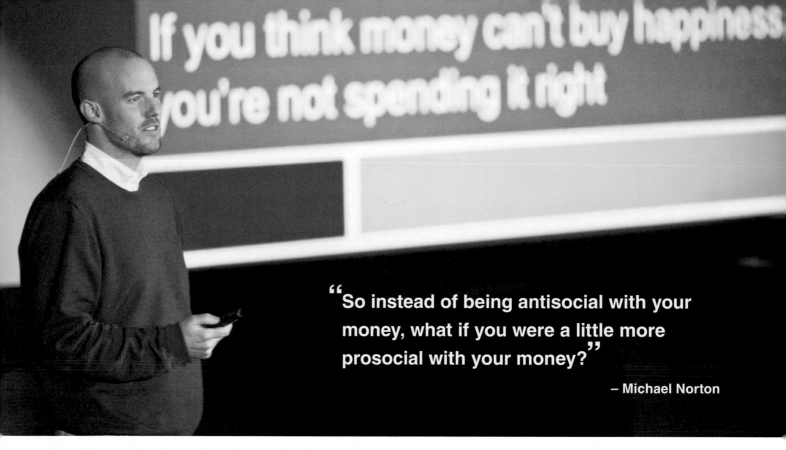

If you think money can't buy happiness you're not spending it right

"So instead of being antisocial with your money, what if you were a little more prosocial with your money?"

— Michael Norton

☐ "In fact, it doesn't matter how much money you spent. What really matters is that you spent it on somebody else rather than on yourself."

What they bought

Personal

Prosocial

☐ "People who spent money on other people got happier. People who spent money on themselves, nothing happened."

And into companies

☐ "One of the teams pooled their money and bought a piñata . . . very silly, trivial thing to do, but think of the difference on a team that didn't do that at all."

And beyond

☐ "The teams that we give the money to spend on each other, they become different teams and, in fact, they dominate the league by the time they're done."

☐ "And so I'll just say, I think if you think money can't buy happiness you're not spending it right."

Listen for Key Information

As you listen, you do not need to focus on every word you hear. Listen for specific words and phrases to get the information you need.

This boy is buying food for his family. How do you think he feels?

After You Watch

A Watch the TED Talk again. Match the information to make sentences about what Michael Norton's experiments suggest.

1. _____ If people on sports teams spend money on themselves,
2. _____ If students spend money on each other,
3. _____ If people on sales teams spend money on each other,
4. _____ If students spend money on themselves,
5. _____ If people on sales teams spend money on themselves,
6. _____ If people on sports teams spend money on each other,

a. they will feel happier.
b. they will not sell more.
c. they will win more games.
d. they will sell more.
e. they will not feel happier.
f. they will not win more games.

B Complete these sentences.

1. To be prosocial with money means to spend it on _____ .

2. People who are prosocial with money often feel _____ and perform _____ at work or at sports.

3. Norton suggests that it is not important how _____ money you spend on others; the benefits are the same.

C 🔁 Work with a partner. Take turns making statements about what you saw in the TED Talk. Your partner says which experiment you are talking about.

D 🔗 Work with a group. Make a list of advice for a person who wants to have a happy and healthy lifestyle. Use what you already knew and what you learned in the TED Talk.

> **You should . . .**

> **You must not . . .**

E 👥 Interview three classmates about the last time they spent money on someone else. Follow the steps below.

- Write a list of questions, using *Who, What, How much,* and *Why.*

Questions	Names		
	_____	_____	_____
1.			
2.			
3.			
4.			
5.			

- Interview your classmates. Ask follow-up questions. Find out how your classmates felt after spending the money.
- Share what you learned with the class. Did what you learned from your classmates match what you learned in the TED Talk?

F 👥 With your group, look at the chart. Think about how you and your group spend money. Can you think of ways to spend money that are more prosocial? Think of a way to spend money that would be more prosocial and share your idea with the class.

Challenge! 👥 Place a check (✓) next to the **four** statements that represent the main ideas of Norton's talk.

_____ Money cannot buy happiness.

_____ Spending money in a prosocial way has a positive effect.

_____ Spending money on others often makes people feel happier, be more productive, and have stronger relationships.

_____ The important thing is to spend money on others—even a trivial amount can have a positive effect.

_____ Winning money makes people happy.

_____ The positive effects of spending money in a prosocial way seem to be the same all over the world.

_____ People should not buy things for themselves.

With a team, pick one idea and talk about ways people can work toward using the idea in their own lives. Come up with a plan of action and share it with the class.

UNIT 1

boring: not interesting

chef: a cook in a restaurant

dancer: a person who earns money by dancing

dangerous: unsafe or harmful

doctor: a professional who helps sick or injured people

engineer: a person who plans the making of machines, roads, and bridges

happy: a joyful or cheerful feeling

interesting: something that is exciting or unusual

journalist: a person whose job is to collect news

photographer: someone who takes photos as a job

pilot: a professional who flies airplanes

police officer: a person who is trained to maintain law and order

politician: a person with a job in politics or government

poor: to not have a lot of money

rich: to have a lot of money

teacher: a person whose job is to instruct and educate others

travel agent: a person who plans trips and holidays

safe: not harmful or dangerous

unhappy: a sad feeling

UNIT 2

brush your teeth: clean your teeth with a small brush

catch the bus: get on a bus on time

celebrate: to do something special, like have a party, to mark an occasion

costumes: clothes worn by a person who is trying to look like a different person or thing

decorate: to make a place or object look beautiful or festive

eat breakfast: eat the first meal of the day, usually in the morning

eat out: eat at a restaurant

festival: a public celebration that takes place on special occasions

fireworks: colorful explosions of light in the sky, usually used for celebrations

fun: a good time

get up: wake up and get out of bed

go to bed: lie down to go to sleep

go to the movies: go to a theater to watch a film

masks: material worn on the face to hide one's identity

present: a gift

start work: begin your job

take a nap: sleep for a short time when it is not time for bed

take a shower: wash under a shower

watch TV: look at a TV

visit friends: go see friends

UNIT 3

airline ticket: a printed piece of paper bought for travel on an airplane

board the airplane: get on the airplane

buy duty free goods: buy goods at a store in an airport that do not add tax to the price

buy your ticket: use cash or credit cards to get a ticket

cash: paper money, like dollar bills, and metal coins used to buy things

check in: arrive and show your ticket

credit cards: a plastic card that allows a person to buy things by borrowing money

claim your baggage: pick up bags or suitcases after a flight

go through customs: when items brought into a country are checked by an official

go through immigration: have government workers check the passports and visas of travelers

go through security: have government workers check travelers to make sure no one has anything dangerous

international driver's license: a document that allows people to drive a car or motorcycle in foreign countries

pack your bags: put clothes and other things in bags

passport: a small book issued by a government to a citizen of a nation for travel

take a taxi: get somewhere using a car with a driver for hire

travel insurance: an agreement with a company in which you pay them money to cover costs and reduce the risk of travel

visa: a document that allows a person to travel to a country

UNIT 4

apple: a round fruit with firm, white flesh

bagel: a piece of bread that is round with a hole in the middle

banana: a long, curved fruit with yellow skin

beans: seeds that can be eaten

breakfast cereal: a breakfast food made from grain

broccoli: a vegetable with green stalks and green or purple heads

butter: soft yellow substance made from cream

cauliflower: large, round vegetable with a hard, white center

cheese: a solid food made from milk

chicken: the meat from a type of farm bird

coffee: a hot, brown, energy-giving drink made by water and coffee beans

customer: someone who buys goods or services

dairy products: different types of food that are made from milk

drinks: liquids that can be swallowed

egg: oval object made by birds, often eaten as food

fiber: a part of a plant found in many fruits and vegetables that is a part of a healthy diet

fish: the meat from an animal with fins that lives in the sea

fruits: the part of a plant that holds the seeds

hamburger: ground meat shaped into a flat circle

juice: a liquid that comes from a fruit or vegetable

lemon: a bright yellow fruit with sour juice

lettuce: a vegetable with large green leaves

meat: the flesh of animals

milk: a white liquid produced by some female animals such as cows

nuts: a fruit with a hard shell or its seed

onion: a round, layered vegetable with light brown skin

orange: a round juicy fruit with orange skin

pepper: a hollow vegetable with seeds inside

potato: round vegetables with white or red skins and white insides

protein: a substance found in meat, fish, and dairy foods that promotes growth

sausage: meat formed into a tube

shrimp: small shellfish with long tails

soda: a sweet carbonated drink

steak: a large piece of meat or fish

tea: flowers and leaves that are dried, shredded, and brewed into a drink

tomato: a soft, red fruit

tuna salad: a food that has chopped tuna meat and vegetables

turkey bacon: salted and smoked turkey meat

vegetables: different plants that can be eaten as food

waiter: a person who serves food and drink in a restaurant

water: clear liquid with no color or taste, people and animals need it to survive

UNIT 5

baseball: a game played on a field by nine players on each team using a small ball and a bat

climbing: a sport where a person moves upward over a vertical surface

diving: a water sport where a person jumps into water

fix the roof: repair the top of a house

football: a sport played by two 11-person teams, using an oval ball. In order to win one must pass or run the ball over the opponent's line

golf: an outdoors game in which people hit a small hard ball into a hole with a stick

go to the movies: (see Unit 2)

gymnastics: exercises that develop strength, coordination, and movement

hiking: taking a long walk in the country or up a mountain

ice hockey: ice-skating sport that uses curved sticks and a small round disk

jogging: running slowly as a form of exercise

lifting weights: a sport in which people try to lift very heavy objects

playing soccer: play a sport of two teams of 11 players, who kick a round ball into goals

skateboarding: a sport where people do tricks on a narrow board with four wheels

study: spend time learning about a subject

swimming: a sport in which people move through water by moving parts of the body

taking a break: taking time to relax

volleyball: a sport played with six players on each side of a net who score points by grounding the ball on the opponents' side

UNIT 6

buy souvenirs: buy objects to remember a place

check into the hotel: arrive at a hotel and get a room

emphatic adjectives: (See page 72)

pack suitcases: to place objects in bags or luggage in order to transport them during travel

unpack suitcases: to remove objects from a bag or luggage

rent a car: to pay money in order to use a car

take a bus tour: go on a bus that will visit places of interest and have a guide

take photos: take pictures with a camera

visit places of interest: go to famous places

bad: unpleasant or harmful

dirty: not clean

e-mail: mail sent over the Internet

fax: a document that is sent electronically through telephone lines

green: the color of grass

hearing: listening to sounds through the ears

letter: a written or typed message sent by mail

loud: intense sound

newspaper ad: a printed advertisement that appears in a newspaper

salty: something that has the taste of salt

sight: the ability to see using your eyes

smartphone: a mobile phone that can access the Internet

smell: the feeling sensed through the nose

social media: websites and applications used for connecting with people on the Internet

soft: nice to touch

sweet: having a taste like sugar or honey

taste: the sense of flavor that comes from the tongue

text message: an electronic message sent through a cellular phone

touch: the ability to feel through the skin, especially with the fingers

TV: box-like device that shows pictures and sounds

wet: covered with, or full of, water or another liquid

buy a new car: pay money to own a car

buy my own house: pay money to own a house

clean the house: to remove dirt and dust from a house

cloudy/overcast: covered with clouds; not sunny

cold/cool: having a low temperature; not warm

do the laundry: wash dirty clothes

get a new job: switch jobs

have children: start a family

hot/warm: having a high temperature; not cold

rain boots: shoes that are worn in the rain, usually made out of rubber or plastic

raincoat: a coat that stops a person from getting wet

rainy/wet: having a lot of rain

scarf: a piece of cloth worn around the neck

speak English fluently: to easily speak or write English

study for the next test: practice, read, and listen to get ready for a quiz

sun hat: a hat that protects the head and neck from the sun

sunglasses: eyeglasses that protect the eyes from the sun

sunny/bright/clear: brightly lit with sunlight; not cloudy

sweater: a warm piece of clothing worn over the upper body

swimsuit: a piece of clothing that is worn to go swimming

umbrella: a folding fabric used to protect someone from rain

windy/breezy: with a lot of wind

belt: a strip of leather or cloth worn around the waist

blouse: a woman's shirt

cheap: goods that don't cost a lot

coat: warm clothing worn over other clothes

cool: a temperature that is low, but not too low

cotton: cloth made from the soft white fiber of a certain plant

expensive: costs a lot of money

gloves: a covering for the hand with separate parts for each finger

handbag: a woman's purse

hat: a clothing item which covers the head

heavy: something that weighs a lot; warm clothing

jacket: a short coat

jeans: informal pants made of denim

leather: animal skin used for clothing

light: something that does not weight a lot; clothing that is not warm

man-made fiber: fibers that are created by people

pants: a piece of clothing that covers the legs

rough: uneven and not smooth

shirt: a piece of clothing worn on the upper body

shoes: a covering for the foot

silk: cloth made from the fibers created by silkworms

skirt: a piece of women's clothing that covers the waist, hips, and part of the legs

smooth: with no roughness or holes

sneakers: a kind of shoe usually worn for sports or casual activities

socks: a piece of cloth worn over the foot and under a shoe

suit: a formal jacket and pants made from the same fabric

tie: a piece of cloth worn by men around the neck for formal occasions

t-shirt: a short-sleeved shirt worn over the upper body

warmth: amount of heat something makes

wool: cloth that is made from sheep's hair

bad shape: not healthy and physically fit

cycling: to ride on a bicycle

eating a balanced diet: eating all of the important food groups

eating lots of sugar: eating foods and drinks that are sweet and unhealthy

good shape: healthy and physically fit

healthy: in good condition; strong, fit, in good shape

heartwarming: something that makes you happy

homegrown: produced in your own garden

homemade: not made in a factory

junk food: food that tastes good but is bad for your health

lifelong: all your life

lifestyle: a way of living

low calorie: not high in calories

mouth-watering: delicious; very good food

overworked: works too much

smoking: the use of tobacco, usually with cigarettes and cigars

stress-free: without worries or problems

sunbathing: to lie out underneath the sun

works out: exercises

watching lots of TV: spend a lot of time watching TV

buy the groceries: purchase food and household things

cut the grass: use a machine to shorten grass

get a credit card: sign up for and receive a credit card

get a promotion: receive an advancement to a new and better job

graduate from high school/college: to receive a degree from an academic institution

iron the clothes: smooth out wrinkles on clothing

pass your driving test: pass an examination given to test a person's ability to drive

pay the bills: pay money for heat, electricity, and other household needs

put away the clothes: clean up and store clothes

run a marathon: run a race of over 26 miles (41.3 km)

sweep the floor: to clear a surface of dust or dirt using a broom or brush

travel abroad: travel out of the country

vacuum: to clean with a vacuum cleaner

walk the dog: to take a dog outside

borrow: to receive something with the promise to return it

budget: an amount of money set aside for a purpose; a financial plan

camel: a large four-legged animal with a long neck and hump(s) on its back

coral reef: hard substance formed from the bones of tiny sea animals

desert: a very dry region with little or no rain

elephant: one of the largest land-mammals, with gray skin, a trunk, and long tusks

expenses: things that must be paid

grasslands: flat land covered with wild grass

income: the amount of money earned from working

interest rates: extra money that has to be paid back when you borrow money

lend: to allow the use of something for a period of time

monkey: a primate with thumbs, long tails, and human-like faces

mountain goat: a four-legged animal with horns that lives on mountains

mountains: a tall formation of land and rock higher than a hill

overspend: to spend too much money

rain forest: a forest with a lot of rainfall that has many different kinds of plants and animals

save: not to spend or use too much money in order to keep some for the future

shark: a meat-eating fish that lives in oceans and large rivers

SKILLS INDEX

COMMUNICATION

GRAMMAR

LISTENING

PRONUNCIATION

READINGS

SPEAKING

giving advice, 33, 40, 125, 126
giving opinions and reasons, 32
job interviews, 139
making predictions, 38, 78, 101
naming objects, 165
role-playing, 32, 37, 47, 65, 105, 116, 139
trip planning, 113, 151

TED TALKS

How to Buy Happiness, 158–161
The Interspecies Internet? An Idea in Progress, 118–121
My Mind-Shifting Everest Swim, 78–81
A Virtual Choir 2,000 Voices Strong, 38–41

TEST-TAKING SKILLS

categorizing, 60
checking off answers, 18, 47, 59, 70, 90, 98, 99, 104, 105, 111, 139, 140, 154, 158, 161
circling answers, 7, 8, 9, 16, 18, 25, 37, 61, 70, 74, 86, 117, 126, 150
completing charts, 19, 31, 41, 76, 86, 87, 92, 101, 111, 120, 127, 132, 145, 151, 159, 161
definitions, 148
fill in the blanks, 4, 5, 6, 9, 13, 18, 49, 57, 61, 65, 69, 71, 77, 78, 110, 117, 118, 145, 157
labeling pictures, 16, 38, 56, 60, 62, 72, 80, 84, 108, 136, 140
matching, 5, 30, 64, 68, 72, 93, 96, 97, 108, 118, 120, 128, 133, 137, 149, 150
multiple choice, 18, 22, 25, 70, 80, 86, 117, 129, 149, 150, 159, 160
ordering pictures, 28
ordering sentences, 157
ranking answers, 116, 144, 157
rewriting questions, 101
sentence completion, 9, 17, 20, 24, 28, 29, 32, 38, 45, 49, 64, 72, 73, 77, 80, 89, 97, 100, 101, 108, 109, 113, 124, 128, 137, 138, 142, 152, 153, 156, 160
sorting answers into columns, 8, 12, 25, 46, 48, 52, 60, 68, 84, 96, 104, 124
true or false, 10, 13, 25, 30, 34, 37, 40, 53, 62, 70, 77, 90, 93, 98, 112, 133, 142, 145
underlining answers, 74, 102, 108
unscrambling sentences, 9, 21, 68, 85, 149
writing requests and predictions, 85, 101
writing questions, 33, 101, 129

TOPICS

Achievements, 134–145
Communication, 82–93
Consequences, 146–157
Destinations, 66–77
Food, 42–53
Going Places, 26–37
Lifestyles, 122–133
Moving Forward, 94–105
People, 2–13
Sports, 54–65
Types of Clothing, 106–117
Work, Rest, and Play, 14–25

VIDEO JOURNAL

Beagle Patrol, 37
Cheese-Rolling Races, 65
Dangerous Dinner, 53
The Last of the Woman Divers, 13
Machu Picchu, 77
Monkey Business, 25
The Missing Snows of Kilimanjaro, 157
The Science of Stress, 133
Solar Cooking, 105
Spacewalk, 145
Traditional Silk Making, 117
Wild Animal Trackers, 93

VOCABULARY

achievements, 140
activities, 56, 58
animals, 152
chores, 136
clothing, 100, 108, 112
communication methods, 84
compound adjectives, 128
countries and nationalities, 4
daily routine, 16
descriptive adjectives, 8
diets, 48
emphatic adjectives, 72
festivals and celebrations, 20
food, 44, 48
habitats, 152
habits, 124
money, 32, 148
numbers, 30
occupations, 4
party words, 20
people, 4
planning, 96
senses, 88
sports, 56, 60
travel, 28, 32, 68
weather conditions, 100

WRITING

advice, 125
answering questions, 64, 116, 132
e-mails, 64, 156
job descriptions, 12
letters, 156
list-making, 13
make suggestions, 156
paragraphs, 24, 76, 104, 116, 132, 144
recipes, 52
statements about the future, 104
text messages, 92
travel blog, 71, 76
travel tips, 36
word webs, 14

ILLUSTRATION

4: (t) National Geographic Maps; 7: (1 to 6) Nesbitt Graphics, Inc.; 8: (lt and lb) Nesbitt Graphics, Inc.; 44: (t) Keith Neely/IllustrationOnline.com; 45: (b) Nesbitt Graphics, Inc.; 46: (c) Nesbitt Graphics, Inc.; 48: (t) Nesbitt Graphics, Inc.; 57: (c) Rob Schuster; 88: (t, tm, m, bm, b) Nesbitt Graphics, Inc.; 92: (b) Rob Schuster; 108: (t) Kenneth Batelman; 151: (b) National Geographic Maps.

PHOTO

Cover Photo: Slow Images/Photographer's Choice/Getty Images

2–3: (c) Sigit Pamungkas/Reuters; 4: (tl) Raul Touzon/National Geographic Creative, (bl) Robert George Young/Photographer's Choice/Getty Images, (tc) Robert Sisson/National Geographic Creative, (tlc) Damien Meyer/AFP/Getty Images, (trc) jochem wijnands/Horizons WWP/Alamy, (tr) Zhang Meng/Xinhua Press/Corbis, (rc) Daj/Getty Images, (br) Paul Bradbury/OJO Images/Getty Images; 6: (tl) © iStockphoto.com/Peter Close, (tr) © iStockphoto.com/shotbydave, (blc) Simon Jarratt/ Fancy/Corbis, (brc) © iStockphoto.com/yelo34; 7: (tr) Roy Toft/National Geographic Creative; 8: (tl) © iStockphoto.com/nicolesy, (tlc) Jupiterimages/Photos.com/Thinkstock, (trc) © iStockphoto.com/JLBarranco, (tr) © iStockphoto.com/diego_cervo, (bl) © iStockphoto.com/H-Gall, (blc) © iStockphoto.com/lmistock, (brc) © iStockphoto.com/Blue_Cutler, (br) © iStockphoto.com/epicurean; 9: (tc) Michael Christopher Brown/National Geographic Creative; 10–11: (rc) Kevin Fleming/National Geographic Creative; 11: (tr) Priscilla Gragg/Blend Images/Alamy, (tc) William Albert Allard/National Geographic Image Collection; 12: (tc) Alex Treadway/National Geographic Creative, (lc) Steve Raymer/National Geographic Creative, (bl) Simon Jarratt/Ivy/Corbis; 13: (tc) Vincent Prevost/Hemis/Terra/Corbis, (rc) He Lulu Xinhua News Agency/Newscom; 14–15: (c) Stringer/Reuters; 16: (tl) © iStockphoto.com/Juanmonino, (tc) © iStockphoto.com/Justin Horrocks, (tr) Bob Scott/Photodisc/Thinkstock, (lc) Keith Brofsky/Photodisc/Thinkstock, (c) Fuse/Getty Images, (rc) Andrea Chu/Photodisc/Thinkstock, (lc) © iStockphoto.com/BartekSzewczyk, (c) ©

iStockphoto.com/avdeev007, (rc) © Monkey Business Images/Shutterstock.com, (bl) Fuse/Thinkstock, (bc) © iStockphoto.com/Rich Legg, (br) © iStockphoto.com/DIGIcal; 17: (br) Joe Raedle/Getty Images; 18: (tc) Adam Crowley/Blend Images/Getty Images; 20: (tc) India Picture/Collage/Corbis, (lc) Jupiterimages/Photos.com/Thinkstock, (bl) Scott Stulberg/Comet/Corbis; 22: (l) Mike Pont/Getty Images Entertainment/Getty Images, (c) Roberto Serra - Iguana Press/Getty Images Entertainment/Getty Images, (r) C Brandon/Redferns/Redferns/Getty Images; 23: (c) James Duncan Davidson/TED, (inset) Gallo Images/Getty Images News/Getty Images; 24: (t) Chad Springer/Corbis, (bl, bc, br) TED; 25: (tc) Narong Sangnak/epa/Corbis Wire/Corbis; 26–27: (c) Kani Polat/500px Prime; 28: (tl) © iStockphoto.com/leezsnow, (tc) © iStockphoto.com/Neustockimages, (tr) © Galyna Andrushko/Shutterstock.com, (lc) © James Steidl/Shutterstock.com, (c) Hemera Technologies/Photos.com/Thinkstock, (rc) Bruno Domingos/Reuters/Corbis, (bl) Digital Vision/Getty Images, (bc) TongRo Images/Harry Choi/Alamy, (br) Timur Kulgarin/Shutterstock.com, (bl) Fuse/Thinkstock; 29: (br) Skip Brown/National Geographic Creative; 30: (tc) Bill Bachmann/Science Source; 31: (tc) Mike Theiss/National Geographic Creative; 32: (tl) © emilie zhang/Shutterstock.com, (tlc) AP Images/Rebecca D'Angelo, (lc) Imagedoc/Alamy, (blc) © Oleksiy Mark/Shutterstock.com, (bl) Martin Shields/Alamy, (c) Andrew Woodley/Alamy, (rc) Alan Myers/Alamy; 33: (br) Andria Patino/Encyclopedia/Corbis; 34–35: (rc) Jimmy Chim/National Geographic Creative; 36: (tc) Pola Damonte/Moment Open/Getty Images; 37: (tc) Lauralea Lasher/National Geographic Creative, (rc) european pressphoto agency b.v./Alamy; 38: (1) © Jonathan Lewis/Shutterstock.com, (2) © criben/Shutterstock.com, (3) © Aschindl/Shutterstock.com, (4) © muzsy/Shutterstock.com; 39: (t) James Duncan Davidson/TED, (bl, br, t) TED; 40: (t) TED; 41: (t) Christian Vorhofer/imagebroker/Corbis; 42: (c) © Lucy Vaserfirer/500px Prime; 45: (cl) © iStockphoto.com/PaulCowan, (b) © iStockphoto.com/Andrea Skjold, (cr) © iStockphoto.com/1 design; 46: (t) Jonathan Kingston/National Geographic Creative; 47: (r) Chris Howes/Wild Places Photography/Alamy; 48: (1) © Dionisvera/Shutterstock.com, (2) © g215/Shutterstock.com, (3) © zcw/Shutterstock.

com, (4) © Gordo25/Shutterstock.com, (5) © iStockphoto.com/jaker5000, (6) © Elena Schweitzer/Shutterstock.com, (7) © iStockphoto.com/alex-mit, (8) © GVictoria/Shutterstock.com; 50: (l) Kevin Foy/Alamy, (inset) f4foto/Alamy; 51: (tr) Dan Kitwood/Getty Images News/Getty Images; 52: (t) Rolf Nussbaumer/imagebroker/Canopy/Corbis; 53: (t) Brian J. Skerry/National Geographic Creative, (1) © Alexius Sutandio/Shutterstock.com, (2) lilithlita/iStock/360/Getty Images, (3) Ben Horton/National Geographic Creative, (4) Ben Horton/National Geographic Creative; 54: (c) Courtesy Tim Kemple; 56: (1) Lear Miller Photo/Image Source/Alamy, (2) © iStockphoto.com/isitsharp, (3) Francesco Tremolada/SOPA RF/Ramble/Corbis, (4) Tim McGuire/Comet/Corbis, (5) © iStockphoto.com/Mari, (6) JGI/Jamie Grill/Blend Images/Getty Images, (7) © oliveromg/Shutterstock.com; 57: (r) Jill Schneider/National Geographic Creative; 58: (tl) © Monkey Business Images/Shutterstock.com, (tc) © Bull's-Eye Arts/Shutterstock.com, (tr) © Diego Cervo/Shutterstock.com, (bl) © Aspen Photo/Shutterstock.com, (bc) Jupiterimages/Stockbyte/Thinkstock, (br) © iStockphoto.com/buckarooh; 59: (t) Michael Hanson/National Geographic Creative; 60: (tl) © Mayskyphoto/Shutterstock.com, (tr) Koki Nagahama/Getty Images Sport/Getty Images, (bl) © Sergey_Peterman/Shutterstock.com, (br) © Nikolpetr/Shutterstock.com; 61: (r) Keith Ladzinski/alex-honnold-MR.pdf/alex-lowthe/Aurora/Passage/Corbis; 62: (tl, tr, bl, br) TED; 63: (t) Darren Staples/Reuters, (c) AP Images/MTI/Peter Komka, 63 (c) James Duncan Davis, 63 (inset) © 7382489561/Shutterstock.com, (b) Ryan Pierse/Getty Images Sport/Getty Images; 64: (t) © iStockphoto.com/DanielPrudek; 66: (c) Jim Richardson/National Geographic Creative; 68: (1) © Konstantin Sutyagin /Shutterstock.com, (2) © iStockphoto.com/Tempura, (3) © iStockphoto.com/ImagesbyTrista, (4) Richard Wong/Alamy, (5) © iStockphoto.com/1001nights, (6) © iStockphoto.com/RiverNorthPhotography, (7) Max Alexander/Dorling Kindersley/Getty Images; 69: (r) Alison Wright/National Geographic Creative; 70: (l) Joseph C. Justice Jr/Getty Images; 71: (t) Beverly Joubert/National Geographic Creative, (b) Dmitry Rukhlenko/Travel Photos/Alamy; 72: (tl) Jamie Grill/JGI/Blend Images/Alamy, (tr) Michael Hanson/National Geographic Creative; 73: (r) Tim Laman/

National Geographic Creative; **74:** (b) Hiram Bingham/National Geographic Creative; **75:** (tr) Hiram Bingham/National Geographic Creative, (c) Micheal Melford/National Geographic Creative; **76:** (t) © WitR/Shutterstock.com; **77:** (t) Johnny's photography/Moment/Getty Images; **78:** (tl) FRANS LANTING/National Geographic Creative, (tr) BORGE OUSLAND/National Geographic Creative, (bl) © 7382489561/Shutterstock.com, (br) MIKE THEISS/National Geographic Creative; **79:** (t) James Duncan Davidson/TED, (bl) MIKE THEISS/National Geographic Creative, (bc, br) TED; **81:** (t) RICHARD OLSENIUS /National Geographic Creative, (tl) RALPH LEE HOPKINS/National Geographic Creative, (tr) MIKE THEISS/National Geographic Creative, (bl) SKIP BROWN/National Geographic Creative, (br) PETE MCBRIDE/National Geographic Creative; **82:** (c) Petra Warner and Wolf Park; **84:** (1) © PaulPaladin/Shutterstock.com, (2) © iStockphoto.com/JaminWell, (3) © Steven Frame/Shutterstock.com, (4) Wavebreakmedia Ltd/Thinkstock, (5) Ingram Publishing/Thinkstock, (6) © Forest Badger/Shutterstock.com, (7) © Feng Yu/Shutterstock.com, (8) © bloomua/Shutterstock.com; **86:** (t) Nicole Duplaix/National Geographic Creative, (l) © StepStock/Shutterstock.com; **88:** (1) © iStockphoto.com/ALEAIMAGE, (2) © Edyta Pawlowska/Shutterstock.com, (3) © iStockphoto.com/cveltri, (4) © iStockphoto.com/jallfree, (5) © iStockphoto.com/Atlanta-Mike, (6) Fuse/Thinkstock, (7) © Monkey Business Images/Shutterstock.com, (8) Michael Blann/Digital Vision/Thinkstock; **89:** (t) David Coleman/Alamy; **91:** (c) James Duncan Davidson/TED; (inset) RALPH LEE HOPKINS/National Geographic Creative; **92:** (t) DAVID DOUBILET/National Geographic Creative; **93:** (t) RALPH LEE HOPKINS/National Geographic Creative; **94:** (c) XPACIFICA/National Geographic Creative; **96:** (1) © iStockphoto.com/Danila Krylov, (2) Top Photo Group/Thinkstock, (3) © iStockphoto.com/asiseeit/Steve Debenport, (4) © iStockphoto.com/Digitalskillet, (5) © iStockphoto.com/joxxxxjo, (6) Andrew Olney/Photodisc/Thinkstock, (7) © iStockphoto.com/YinYang, (8) Fuse/Thinkstock; **97:** (b) cotesebastien/iStock/360/Getty Images; **98:** (l) © MrKornFlakes/Shutterstock.com; **99:** (t) Bill Ross/Comet/Corbis; **100:** (1) © Alexander Shalamov/Shutterstock.com, (2) © Jozsef Szasz-Fabian/Shutterstock.com; (3) ©

iStockphoto.com/Floortje, (4) © Nikolay Postnikov/Shutterstock.com, (5) © iStockphoto.com/Oktay Ortakcioglu, 100 (6) © iStockphoto.com/evemilla, (7) © studioVin/Shutterstock.com, (8) © sunabesyou/Shutterstock.com; **101:** (b) Michael Melford/National Geographic Creative; **102:** (c) MICHAEL MELFORD/National Geographic Creative; **104:** (t) Detlev van Ravenswaay/Picture Press/Getty Images; **105:** (t) Orjan F. Ellingvag/Dagens Naringsliv/Corbis News Premium/Corbis, (1) © vovan/Shutterstock.com, (2) © Alex Kuzovlev/Shutterstock.com, (3) © iStockphoto.com/WendellandCarolyn, (4) © iStockphoto.com/visdia, (5) Medford Taylor/National Geographic Creative; **106:** (c) Amy Toensing; **110:** (t) Cheryl Chan/Moment Open/Getty Images; **112:** (l) © iStockphoto.com/Jitalia17, (cl) © iStockphoto.com/AlexKalina, (c) © sagir/Shutterstock.com, (cr) © iStockphoto.com/itsjustluck, (r) Photos.com/360/Getty Images; **114:** (l) Luis Marden/National Geographic Creative, (r) oytun karadayi/E+/Getty Images; **115:** (c) Jason Edwards/National Geographic Creative; **116:** (t) Keren Su/Terra/Corbis; **117:** (t) Amy White & Al Petteway /National Geographic Creative; **119:** (t) James Duncan Davidson/TED, (bl, bc, br) TED; **120:** (t) AFP/Stringer/Getty Images; **122:** (c) DAVID DOUBILET/National Geographic Creative; **124:** (1) Jamie Grill/The Image Bank/Getty Images, (2) © iStockphoto.com/Silvrshootr, (3) © iStockphoto.com/enad, (4) © Lukasz Fus/Shutterstoc.com, (5) © iStockphoto.com/DanielBendjy, (6) © iStockphoto.com/digitalskillet, (7) © alicedaniel/Shutterstock.com, (8) ArkReligion.com/Art Directors & TRIP/Alamy, (9) © iStockphoto.com/bloodstone; **126:** (1) 101dalmatians/E+/Getty Images, (2) © iStockphoto.com/Brendan McIlhargey , (3) ©iStockphoto.com/lostinbids/jo unruh; **127:** (t) Brigitte Sporrer/Cultura/Getty Images; **128:** (t) Image Source/Getty Images; **129:** (r) Andersen Ross/Digital Vision/Getty Images; **131:** (r) Roberto Defraia - RobMcfrey/Moment/Getty Images, (inset) David McLain/National Geographic Image Collection; **132:** (t) Thomas Barwick/Iconica/Getty Images; **133:** Atlantide Phototravel/Corbis; **134:** (c) John Burcham/National Geographic Creative; **136:** (1) © Monkey Business Images/Shutterstock.com, (2) © katja kodba/Shutterstock.com, (3) © Sonya etchison/Shutterstock.com, (4) © Anne Kitzman/Shutterstock.com, (5) © iStockphoto.com/jwohlfeil, (6) © iStockphoto.com/Tomaz

Levstek, (7) © iStockphoto.com/Klubovy, (8) Andrey Kekyalyaynen/Alamy; **137:** (b) Willie B. Thomas/E+/Getty Images; **138:** (t) IRA Block/National Geographic Creative; **139:** (b) Medford Taylor/National Geographic Creative; **140:** (1) © iStockphoto.com/GlobalStock, (2) Fang Chun Che/Dreamstime.com, (3) © Koh sze kiat /Shutterstock.com, (4) © iStockphoto.com/Gene Chutka, (5) Eric Audras/PhotoAlto/Alamy, (6) wavebreakmedia Ltd/Thinkstock; **141:** (r) © Songquan Deng/Shutterstock.com; **142:** (inset) RICHARD NOWITZ/National Geographic Creative; **143:** (full) Kenneth Garrett/National Geographic Creative; **144:** (t) NASA/National Geographic Creative, (t) Corbis; **145:** (t) NASA/ESA/National Geographic Creative; **146:** (c) Joshua Holko www.jholko.com; **148:** (tl) Jim Richardson/National Geographic Creative, (c) Eric Audras/PhotoAlto/Alamy; **150:** (t) Towfiqu Photography/Moment/Getty Images; **151:** (tr) Marc Moritsch/National Geographic Creative; **152:** (1) © iStockphoto.com/Angel Herrero de Frutos, (2) © kavram/Shutterstock.com, (3, 4) FRANS LANTING/National Geographic Creative, (5) © marcoap1974/Shutterstock.com, (6) © iStockphoto.com/Ammit, (7) Richard Nowitz/National Geographic Creative, (8) © ShaneGross/Shutterstock.com, (9) Michael S. Quinton/National Geographic Creative, (10) © HonzaHruby/Shutterstock.com; **153:** (tr) FRANS LANTING/National Geographic Creative; **155:** (t) Justin Ide/TED, (inset) Pascal Deloche/Godong/Corbis; **156:** (t) Jeremy Woodhouse/Blend Images/Corbis; **157:** (t) Michele Burgess/Photolibrary/Getty Images; **159:** (t) Justin Ide/TED , (l, rt, rc, rb) TED; **160:** (t) Jason Edwards/National Geographic Creative.

TEXT

50–51: Adapted from "Bugs as Food: Humans Bite Back," by Maryann Mott: National Geographic News Public Website, April 16, 2004, **74–75:** "In the Wonderland of Peru," by Hiram Bingham: National Geographic Magazine, April 1913, **102–103:** Adapted from "Powering the Future," by Michael Parfit: National Geographic Magazine, August 2005, **114–115** Adapted from "Silk: The Queen of Textiles," by Nina Hyde: National Geographic Magazine, November 2005, **130–131** Adapted from "New Wrinkles on Aging," by Dan Buettner: National Geographic Magazine, October 1999 All TED Readings are adapted from information either within TED Talks or on the TED website.